Stress Management Skills Training Course

**Exercises and techniques to manage stress and anxiety
Build success in your life by goal setting, relaxation and changing thinking with NLP**

Free downloadable workbook

Kathryn Critchley

Skills Training Course
www.UoLearn.com

Stress Management Skills Training Course

Exercises and techniques to manage stress and anxiety
Build success in your life by goal setting, relaxation and changing thinking with NLP
(Skills Training Course)

Published by: Universe of Learning Ltd, reg number 6485477, Lancashire, UK
www.UoLearn.com, support@UoLearn.com

ISBN 978-1-84937-002-8

Other editions:
ebook pdf format 978-1-84937-026-4
International English version 978-1-84937-024-0

Skills Training Course, Universe of Learning and UoLearn are trademarks of Universe of Learning Ltd.

Photographs by various artists, © www.fotolia.com
Cover photo © Andres Rodriguez, www.fotolia.com

Dedication

I dedicate this book to my parents, Margaret and James Critchley

Who are the two most precious people on this earth to me. They have always encouraged me, given me great confidence in myself, shown me a better path than they were blessed with, picked me up, dusted me down and pointed me in the right direction many, many times and loved me with the deepest love. Thank you for always being there and for helping to create the person I have become. I love you both with all my heart and will be eternally grateful for all you have done for me.

I thank my friends and family, especially my brother Drew, Uncle Chris, Mark, Sam, Liz, Simon and Sal who have encouraged and loved me, been patient with me and supported me during good times and bad.

Also to Ollie who has been my faithful pal for the past 12 years, he's like my little guardian angel and is the best and most faithful friend anyone could be blessed with.

A heartfelt thanks to you all.

Special thanks to:
Jane Howitt for being a part of the initial process and her great encouragement.
Margaret Greenhall for her efforts, ideas and inspiration.
Sally Hayes and Dave Smith for their wonderful photographs.

About the author
Kathryn Critchley,
ReaLife Ltd

With over 14 years' experience of high-pressure sales and management roles in the telecoms industry with organisations such as BT and Orange and over 6 years' experience working for the NHS, Kathryn understands the dynamics of team-building, change management, employee motivation and organisational productivity.

She has provided training, coaching or therapy for organisations such as the NHS, Victim Support and Witness Service, Cisco Systems, Peugeot, British Gas, IBM, Royal Sun Alliance, various councils, schools and universities, and is also a trainer with the CIPD.

Kathryn is passionate about helping people make positive changes and achieve their goals. She achieves remarkable results through seminars and workshops, as well as one to one interventions.

She has over 12 years' experience as a coach, therapist and trainer and a wide range of qualifications, including: Dip Counselling, Master NLP Practitioner, INLPTA NLP Master Practitioner, Cert Hypnotherapy, Dip Hypnotherapy, Hypnotherapy Master Practitioner, Graduate Anthony Robbins Mastery University, Dip Stress Management, Cert Advanced Transactional Analysis, Cert Corporate Consulting, Cert Life Coaching, Dip Performance Coaching, Cert Advanced Life Coaching, Cert NLP Life Coaching.

She has also written Coaching Skills Training Course, see www. UoLearn.com and her website is www.realifeltd.co.uk

In this book she shares some of the knowledge and skills that have helped her to manage her own stress and empowered others to do the same.

Contents

CONTENTS

Disclaimer

Please read this carefully before you start this stress management programme.

The information in this stress management programme is for educational purposes only and is solely the opinion of the author. It is in no way a substitute for medical care from a qualified healthcare professional, and is not intended to diagnose, prescribe, treat, administer, cure or heal any health condition. Neither the publisher nor the author directly or indirectly dispense medical advice, nor do they prescribe any remedies or assume any responsibility for those who choose to treat themselves.

Important cautions

Stress can cause serious health problems. If your health is at risk from stress, or if stress is causing long-lasting unhappiness, you need to see a suitably qualified professional. If this is true for you, DO NOT rely solely on the tools, techniques and advice in this programme – get appropriate professional help.

Always consult your doctor, healthcare professional or nutritionist before beginning any exercise or nutrition plan.
Be sure they are aware of any medication you are taking and any health conditions or symptoms that you have.

Some health conditions can be significant factors in considering which nutrition and exercise programmes are appropriate for you or how they should be adjusted for your unique health profile.

Not all exercises are suitable for everyone and this or any exercise programme may result in injury.

To reduce the risk of injury, never force or strain during exercise. If you experience pain or discomfort during exercise, stop immediately and consult your doctor.

The programme's creators, producers and distributors cannot guarantee that this programme is safe and proper for every individual. For that reason, this programme is sold without warranties or guarantees of any kind.

Any liability, loss or damage in connection with any use of this programme, including, but not limited, to any liability, loss or damage resulting from the performance of the exercises demonstrated here, or the advice and information given here, is expressly disclaimed.

Introduction

Welcome to the Stress Management Skills Training Course – your practical, holistic guide to conquering the damaging stress that's part and parcel of our busy lives.

Stress is all around us and affects us all – but it isn't the same for everyone, and each of us handles it differently. One person's challenging pressure is someone else's debilitating stress. Techniques that work well for you might not be so effective for me. There is no single 'right answer', and that's why we want to help you build your own personal toolbox of stress management skills.

Course Overview

We start this course by taking an in-depth look at stress, exactly what it is and how to deal with it.

We show you how to identify your unhealthy stress, and then give you a number of strategies to help you effectively manage and deal with any areas you want to change.

Remember, not all stress is bad, some stress is good and can be healthy – plus it's often a great motivator.

Throughout the programme we take a holistic approach to stress management and consider both manager and employee in the workplace, as well as how to cope outside work and maintain a healthy work-life balance.

Topics include:

✓ Identifying and fully understanding what stress is

✓ How stress affects our performance, physical body and behaviour

✓ The importance of becoming aware of stress and then taking responsibility by implementing simple strategies to make desired changes to reduce stress

We also look at:

✓ Health, nutrition and supplements

✓ How to keep your body strong and energy high during times of stress

✓ How to avoid illness, a lowered immune system and associated stress symptoms and illnesses

✓ Exercise and relaxation

✓ Calming breathing techniques, quick, easy-to-apply two-minute techniques that you can practise anywhere such as in your car, in a demanding meeting, at the office or at home

Unique approach

Our course is different from most because it lets you take a look at the real reasons you may be stressed and what you and only you can do about it.

Based on various coaching and therapy techniques – including NLP (neuro linguistic programming), CBT (cognitive behavioural therapy) and TA (transactional analysis) – this course allows you to consider all the possible reasons and solutions and make your own conclusions, providing you with your own unique stress management and change strategies.

Although we use many different theories and strategies, we keep it simple, easy to understand and easy to apply.

Successful stress management

Most people point the finger at anyone but themselves when it comes to looking at the causes of their stress. However, we're going to show you how the 'Victim Viewpoint' really doesn't work – and introduce you to techniques that do. By taking a more personal, inward-looking approach you can gain far more control and make far more changes than you can by simply waiting and hoping for the world to change around you.

By the end of this course you'll have a much deeper awareness of how you create your own stress and what you can do about it. You'll discover that around 80 per cent of the stress you currently suffer maybe in your head! You'll also find out what you can do to change it for good.

As part of this unique style of training we'll be looking at your beliefs and your own rule structures. This will allow you to challenge yourself, in a safe environment, to really consider whether you need, or would like to make, a few adjustments to how you think about stress. We'll also walk you through easy restructuring and change processes which will allow you to view things differently and start to make deep, long lasting changes.

The course is a little different, informal and lots of fun. All we ask is that you open your mind, take from the course what is right for you, and enjoy!

Kathryn Critchley

Course Objectives

By the end of this course you will be able to:

✓ Understand exactly what stress and pressure are and their effects both inside and outside of the workplace

✓ Recognise the symptoms of excessive stress in yourself and in others

✓ Have the awareness, knowledge and strategies to deal with stress more effectively

Exercise: Stress I want to change

List below the things that cause you stress and that you want to change during this course.

They can be any area of your life – at work or at home.

Refer back to this list in one month's time to see if you're making effective changes and applying what you've learnt during this course.

Session 1
Stress and Beliefs

"We live longer than our forefathers but we suffer more from
a thousand artificial anxieties and cares. They fatigued
only the muscles, we exhaust the finer strength of the nerves."
Edward George Bulwer-Lytton

Session 1:
Stress and Beliefs

This session introduces two fundamental concepts in understanding how we become stressed:

✓ Our comfort zone

✓ Our beliefs

It looks at the way we operate in all areas of life, how we differentiate between challenges and opportunities, and how we react to them.

You're also introduced to one of the most liberating ideas in stress management:
All beliefs, attitudes and behaviours are learnt.
What's learnt can be unlearnt and replaced with something more useful or successful.

Objectives:

When you've studied this session, you should:

- ✓ be able to explain what the comfort zone is, and how it can both help and hinder performance

- ✓ recognise the limits of your comfort zone and decide whether you need to gently extend its boundaries

- ✓ be able to list some of your empowering beliefs and some of your limiting beliefs

- ✓ be aware that beliefs are NOT set in stone – you can change beliefs that don't work for you

Tools in this session:

- ✓ Comfort zone – understanding how it is a natural human trait to want to avoid change due to fear of the unknown

- ✓ Beliefs – identifying the difference between limiting and empowering core beliefs and their impact upon us

- ✓ Belief cycles – understanding how beliefs spiral and how we convince ourselves of them and add further evidence to justify them

The Comfort Zone

The first concept we are going to take a look at is the **comfort zone**. You've probably heard of the comfort zone but never really considered how big your zone is and whether you're prone to staying within it.

Your comfort zone is where you are fully able, competent and comfortable. It is a job that you can do with your eyes shut or routines of life where you know exactly what you are doing. You may feel slightly challenged now and then, but there's nothing you can't easily handle.

When invited to step outside their comfort zone – or if they're pushed outside – many people react with resistance. This is because of the human fear of failure which, when you look into it more deeply, comes from a desire to be accepted, liked and even loved. When most people 'fail' they feel embarrassed, ashamed, silly or stupid because they feel they can't or couldn't do whatever it was they tried.

So it's understandable if at work, or any area of life where there is change, people react with resistance. Change is the unknown, and if you don't know whether you can do something – especially if you have a 'Be Perfect' driver (see page 36) – you could have fears over whether you can do it, can be a success or even cope. Everyday changes such as new computer or telephone systems, new staff, new jobs, new routines and procedures, new management, merging of departments, sections or whole companies or, on a personal level, exams, weddings, divorce, births, deaths, moving house and so on, are all high on the list of stressors due to change.

How big is your zone?

Are you resistant to change?
If you are, you're causing yourself stress.

Imagine what size a child's comfort zone would be compared to an adult's.

Very young children don't have inhibitions; it's only as we grow older that we learn to feel fear, that we learn what embarrassment is and how to feel silly or stupid. We learn to have an ego. This restricts our ability to have the freedom to learn, grow and be open to change. We're nervous about asking questions for fear of looking silly, or resist trying new things for fear of failure, and we avoid doing anything that may cause us to feel embarrassed.

Get the most from anything in life:

- ✓ Open your mind
- ✓ Lose your inhibitions
- ✓ Be free of fear of failure
- ✓ Be who and what YOU want to be!

By being more fluid and open to change, accepting any fear and dealing with it effectively, you won't only grow your confidence and self-esteem but you'll be free to develop your life with more happiness and less stress.

Stress can be greatly reduced by recognising that change can also be a good thing and focusing on the possible positives from a situation rather than being quick to look at the negatives from a point of fear and therefore resistance.

> Choose to flow with change rather than resist; choose to step out of your comfort zone and grow the size of your comfort zone daily. Aim to have a comfort zone the size of a child's where nothing can faze or worry you, and you will notice a huge difference to the amount of stress you have in your life.

'The greatest discovery of my generation is that a human being can change their life by altering their attitude of mind.'
William James

> Remember – the only failure is not trying again. If we fail at something at least we know what NOT to do next time!

Beliefs

What is a belief?

A belief is a thought, not necessarily a fact. It can be attached to a person's values and can be learnt, accepted, experienced or taught and it can be changed.

'Beliefs can be very strong and can have a significant negative or positive impact on a person's life.' (Fiona Beddoes-Jones)

Your beliefs play an important part in stress management because much of the stress you experience is strongly influenced by your beliefs about a situation, your perception and judgement of how to deal with it, and the resulting emotional impact.

Core Beliefs

Core beliefs are fundamental to how we see the world. They're established from very early on throughout our childhood, learnt from our parents, carers or other significant people around us. (Sue Knight, 2002) When we grow up, we often still carry these beliefs and we don't consider whether they're still healthy with a positive impact on our lives or whether they hold us back from achieving our goals, cause problems in relationships, cause us unnecessary stress, worry and anxiety.

Our beliefs influence and mould our behaviour. They form our 'life script', in the sense that whatever we believe dictates how we respond to the situations and the people we meet in our life.

'If I believe that I will always find a way to succeed,
no matter what I do, I'm more likely to do just that than someone
who believes they can never have what they really want.'
Fiona Beddoes-Jones, 1999

So it pays to make sure our beliefs are empowering and positive!

Empowering positive beliefs

Empowering positive beliefs encourage us to look at what we can achieve and are forward-looking positive statements.
For example:

- ✓ Every cloud has a silver lining
- ✓ Destiny is a matter of choice not chance
- ✓ Failure only occurs when you stop trying
- ✓ The past does not equal the future
- ✓ Big changes begin with small steps
- ✓ Success is learning something you did not already know

Limiting beliefs

These focus on the negative, what we cannot have, and hold us back. For example:

- ✗ No pain no gain
- ✗ Don't blow your own trumpet
- ✗ It's a dog-eat-dog world
- ✗ I want never gets
- ✗ Money doesn't grow on trees
- ✗ Life's a b**** and then you die

Just think them through, for a moment. If you believe in 'no pain no gain', does something always have to hurt to be effective and worthwhile?

> Limiting beliefs can cause a tremendous amount of stress and hold us back from being who and what we would like to be. Also, watch out for conflicting beliefs which can be confusing and another great stressor.

What if you want to become wealthy but believe 'money is the root of all evil'? Do you think you would become wealthy? If you did succeed, do you think you would retain your wealth if it signified evil to you?

When I was studying to be a coach the first thing I was asked was 'What do you want? What are your goals?' I realised I had a conflicting belief as what immediately popped into my mind was 'I want never gets'. Therefore, if I said what I wanted, I would never get it! I wasn't even aware of this consciously – it was an **unconscious belief** that presented itself and caught me by surprise.

Common Limiting Beliefs

Here are some common limiting beliefs we hear from our clients.
Tick the ones that apply to you.

- ❑ I can't do that..........
- ❑ I have to eat everything on my plate........
- ❑ Taking time for myself is selfish............
- ❑ I'm too fat/not fit enough to go to the gym.....
- ❑ I can't do it as well as others can....
- ❑ I must be the perfect parent/partner
- ❑ I don't like to say no, its not nice
- ❑ I need cigarettes/chocolate/caffeine/alcohol/drugs to get me through it/help me to relax......

What's really happening when you believe statements like this?
Let's examine some of them more closely.

'I have to eat everything on my plate':
A common childhood learned belief which had some merit
when our parents were keen to get us to eat properly. However,
today's plate sizes are somewhat bigger and a belief such as this,
whether on a conscious or unconscious level, could cause issues.
Many of our clients with weight issues have similar beliefs or
rules.

'I don't like to say no; it's not nice' and 'taking time for myself is selfish': Both common beliefs for people who find it difficult to say 'No'. But by over-committing, you run the risk of doing nothing properly and becoming exhausted.

'I must be the perfect partner/parent/manager/friend/person': Beliefs that ensure a constant battle for something that doesn't and never will exist. Far more likely to cause stress, upset, conflict, jealousy, guilt and many other negative emotions.

'I need cigarettes/alcohol/drugs/coffee to get me through it/help me relax': Things that people convince themselves help during times of stress. In fact, these actually make an uncomfortable state worse by further stressing mind and body.

Challenging limiting beliefs

Everyone has a mixture of beliefs, some empowering and some that are disempowering. You're not doomed to failure just because you hold some limiting beliefs. Don't forget – all beliefs can be changed, reframed, discarded or strengthened if you choose to address them.

Imagine believing that 'destiny is a matter of choice and not chance'. How much control does that give you over making your own decisions in life? Does it make you feel that you are in charge of your own destiny?

Once you recognise limiting beliefs, you then have the power to change them.

> Many of our clients come to us carrying their past traumas around with them, like huge dirty bin bags of rubbish they would like to be free from. Yet constantly focusing on them and bringing them forward with them throughout their life only continues the pain. To believe that 'the past does not equal the future' allows people to accept and deal with the past, yet understand that the future is a whole different thing, that they are free to have their future however they choose.

Take some time to think of some limiting beliefs that you have and list them below. Remember, the first few are not the core ones. Think hard and dig deep for the hidden limiting beliefs you hold which may rule you, even on a subconscious level. We'll come back to this list later during the course and show you how you can change or discard any limiting belief you no longer need or want to keep.

Exercise: My limiting beliefs

Empowering and disempowering belief cycles

Beliefs don't exist on their own. They affect each other, build on each other, becoming stronger and stronger. Create a belief cycle, get those beliefs linked and working on each other, and the whole is greater than the sum of the individual parts.

Unfortunately, that works for disempowering beliefs as much as for empowering ones. Get negative beliefs feeding on each other, and you can be on a downward spiral.

To see how this works, let's consider the build-up to taking an exam. What goes on in someone's head can strongly influence how they perform.

Look at the difference between the following two cycles. Which would you tend to be?

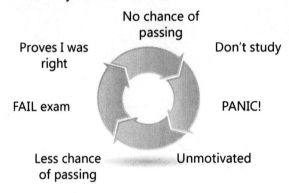

No chance of passing

Don't study

PANIC!

Unmotivated

Less chance of passing

FAIL exam

Proves I was right

Belief – I don't have much chance of passing

- ✗ I don't bother to study much because there isn't much point
- ✗ I know what will happen. I will panic during the exam as they will be the questions I don't understand and it will be really difficult. I will feel embarrassed and stupid and not pass the exam nor get the job.
- ✗ I feel unmotivated
- ✗ I don't sleep or eat well because I am worried
- ✗ I decrease my chances of passing
- ✗ I fail the exam
- ✗ I prove my belief to myself

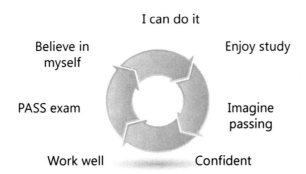

Believe in myself · I can do it · Enjoy study · Imagine passing · Confident · Work well · PASS exam

Belief – I have the potential to pass the exam

- ✓ I study and enjoy the process because there is a purpose to it
- ✓ I can imagine myself passing the exam. I can see myself smiling and receiving my certificate. I'm enjoying knowing that I have passed with the grade I wanted.
- ✓ I feel confident
- ✓ I put my full attention into the exam
- ✓ I work well
- ✓ I pass the exam
- ✓ I prove my belief to myself

Whatever the 'truth' of the matter, both become self-fulfilling prophesies.

Notes:

Personal reflection – stress and change, the fear of change

During the past 11 years of running a therapy and coaching practice I have noticed that regardless of our personality, age, occupation, position, location, financial situation, skills and knowledge, EVERYONE fears change. When we discussed the comfort zone at the beginning of this session we talked about the need to embrace change to be able to flow with the everyday changes that life throws at us. But is this easier said than done? How do we stop fearing it?

The trick is accepting that it is okay to fear change and pushing ahead through the fear regardless. For most people, including myself, it is the fear of failure which often encourages us to resist and avoid issues or prevents us from trying in the first place. There is so much learning to be found in failure, it's a natural process for us to fail and then learn by trying another way. I defy you to identify just one famous inventor or successful person who has not failed many times in order to succeed. It's a natural part of life and makes us who we are and enables us to grow and develop as people and as a society. So, why are we so intent on avoiding failure? Maybe, if we were taught that it's okay to get things wrong at school and encouraged to look at how we define 'wrong' or 'failure' then it wouldn't be such a strong driver for us to avoid.

I guess for most of us it's about re-educating ourselves to be at ease with getting things wrong and then using the experience to get it right in our own way without worrying about our ego and the effect of others' judgements or perceptions. The important part is how we think about our development. If more people were able to embrace this as a positive belief then they would be open to accepting change and trying new things. Remember a lot of this fear can be unconscious thoughts as well as conscious and it is a great way to protect ourselves, yet many people over-protect themselves which then becomes a hindrance.

Just accepting and understanding why we fear change and that it's normal is a huge step in conquering the fear. Then all you need to do is take a deep breath, put your ego and judgements to one side, push through the fear and do it anyway. Whatever happens you will learn something new, and if you start with that as your outcome, then you can only succeed.

Session 2

The Nature of Stress

"Sometimes it's important to work for that pot of gold. But, other times, it's essential to take time off and to make sure that your most important decision in the day simply consists of choosing which colour to slide down on the rainbow." Douglas Pagels

Session 2:
The Nature of Stress

Pressure plays an important role in all areas of life. A certain amount helps to encourage you to get the most out of yourself; but too much can be counter-productive and disabling.

In this session we look at stress in detail: what it is; what causes it and the difference between good and bad stress and how it affects our performance. We also focus on our thinking patterns and show how errors in thinking can undermine our best endeavours.

Objectives:

After working through this chapter you should:

✓ see that there is a difference between motivating pressure and disabling stress

✓ be aware of some of the main causes of stress and list any that are causes of your stress at home and at work

✓ recognise the personal stressors at work in you and the people around you

✓ be able to identify how stress is affecting your performance and whether you need to do anything about it

✓ make a start on making realistic changes by recognising what you can change, what you can influence, and what you cannot change

Tools in this chapter:

✓ Definition of stress – ensure you fully understand what stress is and is not

✓ Personal stressors – to consider how we can cause our own stress and also project stress onto others

✓ The stress curve – to understand the varying degrees of stress, optimum levels and the extremes of too much and too little pressure

✓ Stress audit – assess your own stress levels and causes over a 2 week period

✓ Errors in thinking – understand different thinking patterns and implications

✓ Making realistic changes – identifying areas you can change/ cannot change or could influence

What is stress?

The Health and Safety Executive (www.hse.gov.uk) define stress as:

'The adverse reaction people have to excessive pressure or other types of demands placed on them.'

Although a certain level of pressure is required and healthy, when levels become too high and you cannot cope or you don't have the resources to cope, then your health and efficiency are affected.

As you saw in session 1, operating outside your comfort zone can cause stress because that's when you're likely to be beyond your known range of capabilities or experience.

The answer to managing stress, therefore, seems obvious:

✓ reduce personal demands

✓ avoid change

✓ encourage people to work less

✓ stay in the comfort zone

✓ allow flexible working hours

✓ make more resources available

This solution could work, but it's unrealistic and may be somewhat boring and limiting. This causes problems of its own. Research indicates that too little pressure of any kind leads to under-stimulation, poor performance and boredom. (Jeff Davidson, 1999)

So if we're going to perform at our best, it's essential that everyone is subject to a certain amount of pressure. The trick is to harness the positive pressures caused by demands but to also make available the requisite resources to achieve the right balance between demands and resources.

How we respond

The way we respond physically and emotionally to stress has a major impact on our quality of life, ability to perform at work and our emotional well-being.

The immediate response is innate. Our ancestors relied on it to protect themselves, and it can be seen in nature, too. When confronted with a dangerous situation, the two options are face the challenge or run away. This is called the 'fight or flight response', and it's one we all experience. It's not always a bad experience; it can prepare us for challenging new situations. (We examine the fight or flight response in session 3.)

Stress isn't a weakness, nor is it a strength. It is unique to the individual. Some people can cope with more and some with less. It's important to accept that we are all different and not to judge others by your own ability to cope. It's about finding each person's unique point of balance and working with that, especially if you're in a management role.

Stress connections

Stress isn't just present in the workplace, either. It can occur in all areas of our lives – and all of these areas are interlinked:

➢ Work

➢ Health

➢ Finances

➢ Family

➢ Relationship

Also remember, as a manager you may or may not be aware of personal issues which are affecting an individual's work. It's important to know your boundaries. If you suspect there are personal or hidden issues that need to be dealt with, ensure you refer the person for help or suggest they seek help via an Employee Assistance Programme (EAP), Occupational Health or private therapy/coaching. Often, trying to help with personal issues if you are not qualified can make things worse and conflict with your role as a manager.

It's common to take work issues home, but note that you can take home issues into work, too. Financial problems can affect your health, health issues can affect your family, and relationship issues can affect your finances, and so on. Having issues that cause stress in one of these areas can be difficult to manage, but if you add some problems from the other areas too, or allow unmanaged stress to create stress in connected areas, it can soon add up to one big issue of significant stress.

Causes of stress

Some of the main causes of stress:

➢ Marriage
➢ Divorce
➢ Death
➢ Moving house
➢ End of a relationship
➢ Money issues
➢ Birth
➢ Serious health issues
➢ Family
➢ Redundancy or loss of job
➢ Change of job
➢ Retirement
➢ Overworked
➢ No exercise

Exercise: List some of the current causes of stress in your life.

At home

....
....
....
....
....

At work

....
....
....
....
....

Personal stressors

The concept of 'Personal Stressors' – unrealistic expectations we have of ourselves – provides a useful framework for identifying stress in ourselves and in others, and gives us some knowledge about reducing this stress. It comes from the idea that early in life we develop 'life scripts' – fixed beliefs of how our lives should be. We then continue to 'act out' the distinctive patterns of behaviour that come with our life script.

When these scripts become limiting they are **often the cause of negative stress.**

Personal life scripts are developed from the way parents and significant others transmit values, beliefs and standards to their children in a variety of ways:

➤ By direct instruction – 'You must be kind to people.'

➤ By modelling behaviour to us – 'Mum looks after the family.'

➤ By rewarding or punishing certain behaviours – 'Well done, you didn't cry.'

These messages are often picked up as rules and they become fixed in behaviour patterns. When we're operating in our comfort zone, it's easy to make rational decisions about whether these rules are valid and applicable to the current situation. When we're stressed, however, these rules somehow gather more credence and become almost mandatory.

Rigid and limiting, they become personal stressors, defining the way our lives 'should' be rather than what they could be and increasing our stress.

Common types of personal stressor

The five main personal stressors come from beliefs that we need to be – or we find some perceived value in being – perfect, strong, helpful, stubborn and busy. Of course, there are more personal stressors than these; but these five appear to be the most commonly used. Following are examples of these behavioural types, showing how they stress the individual and also how they pollute emotional environments by spreading individual stressors, expectations and behaviours within work or their home life, negatively affecting or stressing others.

Need to be perfect

'Need to be perfect' has a tendency to feel that they always have to exceed expectations or get things completely, perfectly right. Everything they do has to be a 'Rolls Royce' job – anything less than perfection is a failure. They find it difficult to delegate as they cannot trust anyone else to do the job as well as themselves. They would rather do it themselves than risk it being anything less than an excellent job. They may be causing their self and others unnecessary stress by imparting the stressors onto those around them.

Have to be strong

'Have to be strong' has many positive qualities including being self-sufficient, reliable and undemanding of others. However, the downside tends to be a difficulty in expressing emotion and in seeking help when they really need it. They always appear to cope so well that often people won't even realise that they need help or support. As with 'need to be perfect', they may find delegation difficult since it implies that they are unable to cope.

Always be helpful

'Always be helpful' has been brought up to believe that they must put the needs of others before themselves. If they don't, then they feel they are being selfish. They have even been known to go out of their way to please people they didn't really know that well in addition to their own family and friends. Sometimes they are unable to cope with all the demands of others and need to put themselves first. Always pleasing others can mean that they sometimes lose track of what actually pleases them and lose sight of their own needs and values.

Should be stubborn

'Should be stubborn' often find themselves trying all sorts of things, even those that don't really interest them but they think they should at least have a go at. They are also inclined to stick doggedly to a lost cause at times, rather than giving up because it will be seen as a failure by others. This inability to discriminate and take control may lead to them spending a lot of time doing things that don't interest them, to the detriment of other things that they find fulfilling and exciting.

Must be busy

'Must be busy' needs to feel that if their days are not action-packed from morning till night, if they aren't rushed off their feet, dealing with several jobs at a time, then they just aren't doing enough. They are always thinking and planning their next job before they've finished their current one, they often show impatience with others' 'slowness'. Delegation may be difficult because nobody else can do it as quickly as they can. When they do delegate, they get frustrated if people don't keep pace.

Exercise: Which personal stressors describe you best?
How do they contribute to your stress levels?

Good and Bad Stress

Stress can be good if you are balanced. That is, you have enough healthy stress to stretch and challenge yourself, and you've also got the resources to cope sufficiently.

When looking at the balance of stress, it often helps to imagine a set of old-fashioned scales. The aim is to have enough on each side to maintain balance.

Too little stress can lead to an imbalance and perhaps boredom, lack of motivation, frustration, possibly depression or feeling useless.

Too much stress, on the other hand, tips the scales the other way, leading to being overwhelmed, unable to cope with the volume, feeling helpless, angry, confused and even burnt out.

Identify your stress

The first crucial step in dealing with stress is to be able to identify where you are and see the stress around you. If you can't recognise unhealthy stress, how can you do anything about it? Often, people who don't recognise they are stressed, or make excuses not to deal with it, keep pushing themselves until their mind and body have had enough. The body is very resilient, but eventually the stress will cause a whole range of physical and mental problems and finally burn out.

By understanding your personal stress tolerance levels, and recognising the symptoms of excessive stress, it's possible to develop strategies to help you manage stress. By learning and practising these strategies, it's possible to live the life you desire and improve your quality of life.

Burn out is not a good place to be and can have long-term effects and it also takes time to recover. It's not a couple of weeks off work – it can take months and even up to a few years to fully recover, depending on how the stress has affected your mental and physical health.

A holistic approach focuses on a looking at all areas of coping with stress, such as:

➢ Awareness

➢ Accepting responsibility

➢ Positive attitude

➢ Being open to change and actively creating change

➢ Creating a supportive and realistic belief structure

➢ Healthy diet

➢ Hydration

➢ Relaxation

➢ Exercise

Stress versus Performance

The following stress curve clearly shows how changes in stress affect how we perform.

➤ When demands are too low we can feel depressed and bored.
➤ As pressure increases we become more lively and our performance improves.
➤ The dotted line in the centre is the perfect **BALANCE POINT** – the optimum place to be, where the scales are balanced and all is functioning well. This is what you need to aim for if you're not already there.
➤ But then, as more and more demands are made, our performance deteriorates.
➤ And at its worst, comes **burn out**.

Use the stress curve to gain awareness of where you are now. Then you can decide what you want to do about it.

If you're on the left side with too little to do and feeling under-utilised or under-valued, then what can you do to move more towards the optimum? What have you not done? Who can you ask for help or influence differently to assist you?

If you're on the right side with too much to do and feeling overworked and over-burdened, what can you do to move more towards the optimum? What have you let slip? Why are you there? How can you change things or enlist someone to help you?

If you're at the optimum, how did you get there?
How are you going to maintain it? Examine your strategy to
make sure you don't start to slip over time.

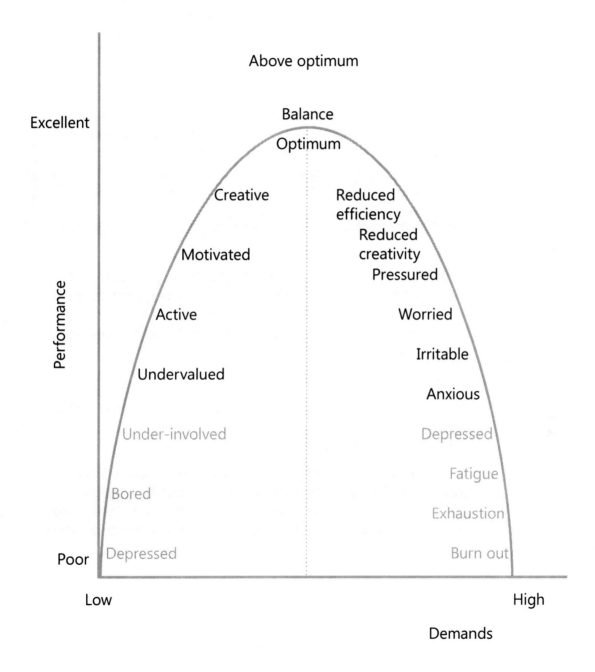

This stress curve can be used as a snapshot of your life or for specific situations, so play around with it and gain awareness of exactly where you are right now, where you have been and where you plan to be. Things can change quickly and you could be at different places along the curve in just one day, which is why we tend to use it for a general snapshot of the whole. Don't worry too much if the words don't fit you exactly; words are just a label and mean different things to different people. They are there as a guide only.

> The danger if you're working at above optimum balance for a prolonged period of time without actively managing your stress is that you can plummet very quickly towards burn out rather than gradually declining over time. So awareness and action is the key.

There are times when you'll need to go above your optimum balance (shown as ABOVE OPTIMUM on the diagram), perhaps when you have a presentation to do, an exam, an interview to prepare for or when you're working longer hours to cover for other job roles.

There are also personal times such as marriage, moving house, birth, death, exams, divorce and so forth, where extra time, preparation or pressure is applied.

During these times it's important to plan and manage your stress. Even if it's something you didn't choose to happen or didn't foresee, ensure you plan some time out, get more sleep, eat well, exercise or relax and apply any of the stress tools you'll learn during this course.

Exercise: Where am I on the stress curve?

....

....

....

Why am I there?

....

....

....

....

....

....

Where do I want to be?

....

....

....

....

....

....

How can I get there?

....

....

....

....

....

....

Stress Audit

To get a good picture of how you're dealing with stress at the moment, keep a personal learning journal for about two weeks. Focus on your feelings, your performance and the stress or pressure around you.

Your journal should give you an audit of your stress levels. If you visit www.UoLearn.com you can download a copy of the stress audit diary.

Routine Stress

At a regular interval, for example every hour, make a note of:

➢ the time
➢ the amount of stress that you feel on a scale of 1 to 10
➢ how happy you feel on a scale of 1 to 10
➢ whether you're enjoying what you're doing
➢ how efficiently you're working

Specific Stress

Each time you experience a stressful event, write down:

➢ what the event was
➢ when and where it occurred
➢ what the fundamental cause of the event was
➢ how stressful the event was on a scale of 1 to 10
➢ how you handled the event
➢ whether you tackled the cause or the symptom
➢ whether you dealt with the stress correctly

Analysis

Over time you'll begin to see patterns emerge:

➢ which of your stress causing behaviours crop up again and again
➢ which external stressors cause you the most difficulty
➢ what triggers these stressors
➢ which events cause you the most stress and which the least

You'll also get a good grasp of whether your current strategies for handling stress are effective or not, and whether you need to implement new techniques.

A blank stress audit document can be downloaded from www.UoLearn.com Here we've just shown the header for the diaries. Keep a track of the things that cause you stress over a week to help you decide your priorities for tackling the causes of your stress.

Stress audit diaries

Routine stress

Fill in every hour to get an overview of the level of stress around you.

Time	How stressed do you feel (1 to 10)?	How happy you feel (1 to 10)?	Are you enjoying what you're doing?	How effectively are you working (1 to 10)?

Specific stress

Fill this in each time you experience a stressful event.

The event	Where and when	Fundamental cause of the event	How stressful was it (1 to 10)?	How did I handle it, was it the right thing to do?	Did I tackle the cause or the symptom?

Errors in Thinking

As with our beliefs and behaviours, thinking patterns can also cause us to feel under pressure and stressed. These are often thought patterns we learn and are caught up in, as we've practised them over and over, so that when triggered they are a set response. These thought and response patterns can be broken. (Rian E McMullin)

> Once you're aware of the process, you can challenge the irrational links, thoughts and beliefs with rational thoughts and questioning techniques. As you disrupt and break the pattern, you can choose and practise new beliefs.

Following are some examples of faulty thinking processes and examples of how irrational thoughts can lead to stress in you and others.

'Should' statements

Should, ought and must are all powerful words and create an instant feeling in your body. These are words which easily create stress and guilt if not followed. Consider the following statements:

➤ I must be on time
➤ I should go to the gym
➤ I ought to ring her
➤ I should be finished by 6pm
➤ I should be in work early
➤ I must do more
➤ I ought to do more
➤ I should be on a diet

Feel how disempowering these words are.

Now re-read all the statements inserting the word **'could'** instead of 'ought' and 'should'.

➤ I could be on time

➤ I could go to the gym

➤ I could ring her

➤ I could be finished by 6pm

➤ I could be in work early

➤ I could do more

➤ I could be on a diet

How different does it feel? How much more in control are you? Now you have a choice and are empowered to choose without the need for pressure or guilt. Try it – it's very simple and it works. Whose rules were they anyway?

Remember perfection doesn't exist!

Exaggerating

Often, people take a small issue or problem and build it up in their mind to make it appear to be much bigger than it is. Then, when they talk about it and picture it, they enlarge it further, until it's so big it's overwhelming and they can't cope. It is important to remain realistic and rational.

If a problem is large, break it into smaller more manageable chunks and take control.

Jumping to conclusions

This is the way to blow things or issues completely out of proportion and cause yourself and others unnecessary stress. How do you know? What evidence do you have? Have you asked other people involved what they think or just assumed something in your head?

Find out the facts before making a decision or judgment and don't assume anything!

Over-generalising

Similar to exaggerating, over-generalising is often done within a person's mind and not based on rational facts. One negative experience does not mean it will always be so. Paranoid and negative thinking are common problems. Your imagination may allow the irrational thoughts to grow enough to become a belief and cause stress and fear.

Catastrophising

Assuming that the worst possible thing is actually going to happen, small issues become disasters. For example, when you have a row with your boss you assume that you're going to lose your job, you'll have to sell your house and you'll never be able to work again.

All-or-nothing thinking

Seeing things in black or white rather than all the shades of grey in between.

The habit of self-blame

This is when you blame yourself for everything whether it's your fault or not. You constantly apologise to people and worry that you may fall out of favour with them or upset them. Seeing everything as your fault means that you're not allowing others to take responsibility for themselves and that you're trying to control them as well as yourself – which, of course, you will never be able to do. Nor will you be able to please everyone all of the time.

Personalisation

This is another paranoid and irrational thought process where you take everything personally. If someone makes a comment about not liking a situation, you take it that they meant they didn't like you. Another aspect of this negative thinking habit is if you constantly compare yourself to others. The result will also always be negative: you're not as good looking, clever, thin, happy, rich, strong and so on as them.

Mind reading

Mind reading is deciding something is true with no evidence – believing that how someone looked at you, or the tone in their voice, means something. For example, they looked bored when you were talking during the meeting. The truth could have been that although they looked bored to you, that facial expression for them was one of concentration as they were trying to take in all the details.

Don't jump to conclusions or make assumptions. If in doubt ask to clarify the facts.

Perfectionism

A thinking process that will always lead to disappointment and negative emotions, as perfection is impossible to achieve and maintain. Setting impossibly high standards is generally a learned behaviour pattern and about pleasing others or proving something.

Perfect doesn't exist; good enough for the job, does.

Selecting the negative and ignoring the positive

This is about dwelling exclusively on the negative aspects of situations and ignoring the positive aspects, as if they don't count. For instance, if you give a presentation which on the whole went well, although a couple things didn't go as well as they could, you might ignore all the good things and think only of the things that went wrong.

Exercise: Do you recognise any of these thinking errors in yourself?

List some instances below:

....

....

....

....

....

....

....

....

....

....

Making Realistic Changes

You may feel that there are parts of your life you'd like to change. You may decide to alter the amount of pressure in your life if you're not completely happy with your pressure balance. Of course, you may be quite happy with things as they are – but when we really want to change, we often stay in the old rut.

Why is it so difficult to change?

➢ I've got too much on at the moment

➢ That's just not me

➢ I'll start tomorrow

➢ I don't have any time for that right now

➢ It costs too much

➢ I can't do it

Do any of these responses sound familiar?

The truth is that change can be challenging. It requires time and energy that we don't always have or we're not always prepared to find. Sometimes change is hindered because of things out of our control.

Therefore, it's useful to determine the things that you can and cannot change so that you can channel your energy appropriately.

Being realistic about change

Exercise: realistic change

Things that affect me/cause me stress that I cannot change are:

....
....
....
....
....

Things that affect me/cause me stress that I can influence are:

....
....
....
....
....

Things that affect me/cause me stress that I can change are:

....
....
....
....
....

Personal Reflection – The importance of spotting the signs and being proactive in managing stress

Stress manifests in many ways and spotting it in time to be proactive rather than reactive is generally the challenging part. How do we know when we are about to become stressed so we can do something about it before it's too late?

We discussed the stress curve during this session considering how either side of having too little to do and too much to do can both cause high levels of stress. We also looked at the optimum, above optimum and burn out. One of the reasons I am so passionate about stress management is because I have suffered with stress myself and know first hand how challenging that can be. Unfortunately, I did not have the awareness you now have and I continued with high stress levels until one day I was no longer able to function mentally or physically and I hit burn out with a major bump. This is not a place I ever wish to return to as it is a dark and painful place and one that takes a significant amount of recovery to get back on your feet. Having hit burn out and having had to find ways to help myself I soon learned how to spot the signs of stress and that slippery path far before the danger zones and am now able to be proactive. This doesn't mean that I never suffer from stress, we all do, it's normal and natural, it just means that I have my own strategies and skills that I've gathered along the way to deal with stress effectively.

Proactively spotting the signs of stress in yourself and doing something about it empowers you as you are in control of your life. Once we have suffered with too much unnoticed or ignored stress and we get into the danger zone of burn out, recovery is a very reactive approach where you are forced to act and are definitely not in control, the stress controls you. I cannot stress enough (pardon the pun) how important it is to spot the signs of stress early on. Some of it may be good stress which is great, use it to perform and motivate yourself. However, if you spot any stress which may have a negative impact on you act quickly. Even some of the small exercises in the programme can have profound and powerful impacts upon people, assisting them with their awareness or managing their chosen levels of stress. Ensure that you remain in the driving seat and take a strong proactive approach to managing stress in your life. Learn from past mistakes where you may have become stressed and recognise what works for you. Make sure you have your eyes wide open to the signs, always act upon them and act as early as possible.

The next session, session 3 will give you specific information of how to spot the signs and symptoms of stress in yourself and others.

Session 3
Recognising Stress

"The time to relax is when you don't have time for it."
Jim Goodwin and Sydney Harris

Session 3:
Recognising Stress

Recognition of a problem is the first step toward creating any solution, so in this session we'll examine the signs and symptoms of stress – what to look out for in yourself and other people.

The main aim is to help you understand the physiological, psychological and behavioural changes stress brings, and give you the opportunity to evaluate your current stress levels.

Objectives:

When you've worked through this session, you will be able to:

✓ tell the difference between signs and symptoms of stress

✓ explain why the fight or flight response can be more damaging than protective under certain conditions

✓ recognise signs of adrenal stress

✓ identify foods, drinks and chemicals that make adrenal stress worse so you can avoid them in times of stress

✓ identify foods that will help

✓ rate how your personality type deals with stress at home and at work

✓ start to identify changes you might want to make

✓

Tools in this chapter:

✓ Signs and symptoms of stress – learn to identify the performance and behavioural changes that can occur

✓ Fight or flight – recognising the natural human response to perceived stress and danger

✓ Adrenal stress and fatigue – awareness of dangers of prolonged unmanaged stress, plus how to spot the signs

✓ How do you cope with stress questionnaire – complete to assess your current coping mechanisms and personal view of stress

✓ Personality types A and B in relation to stress at work questionnaire discover how you behave at work and how you create or manage your stress levels

Signs and Symptoms of Stress

Signs: What you can see in yourself and others.

Symptoms: Subjective experience – what you feel.

It is important to be able to identify the signs of stress in yourself and others and recognise the symptoms of stress in yourself. Remember, everyone is different, so you will have your own unique pattern of signs and symptoms. Learn to spot these quickly so you can take action to effectively manage or deal with stress.

If you're aware of stress and can understand it and if you can identify when it's happening, then you'll be able to manage stress by applying the best strategies for you.

Following are some of the behavioural, performance and physical signs and symptoms of stress. Remember that although these are associated with stress, that they can also be caused by other conditions. Especially with physical symptoms, you must consider all possible underlying reasons and seek medical help to eliminate other likely causes.

Behavioural changes

- ➢ Being irritable or on a short fuse
- ➢ Can't relax or take holidays
- ➢ Ringing into work from holiday
- ➢ Social withdrawal and self-pity
- ➢ Increased swearing and unacceptable language
- ➢ Increased smoking or alcohol consumption
- ➢ Loss or increase of appetite or changes in eating patterns
- ➢ Being unreasonable or aggressive
- ➢ Loss of sense of humour
- ➢ Emotional and easily reduced to tears
- ➢ Prone to accidents
- ➢ Making mountains out of molehills
- ➢ Less effort or concern with appearance
- ➢ Increased/decreased sex drive
- ➢ Nervousness
- ➢ Depression
- ➢ Changed sleeping patterns
- ➢ Insomnia
- ➢ Boredom

Exercise: Add your own specific behavioural changes.

....

....

....

Performance changes

➤ Difficulty in concentrating

➤ Failure to prioritise

➤ Putting things off

➤ Less will or ability to make decisions

➤ Loss of confidence

➤ Undue deference or hostility, antagonism towards senior colleagues

➤ Cynicism and isolationism

➤ Expressing inadequacy and/or insecurity

➤ Become antagonistic or introverted

➤ Keeping things to yourself

➤ No acknowledgement of performance of others

➤ Reduced quality and quantity of work – more errors from less output

➤ Reduction in measured performance outputs

➤ Absenteeism

➤ Changed attitudes to policies and procedures

➤ Poor performance

➤ Time-keeping issues

Exercise: Add your own specific performance changes.

Physical changes

- ➤ Headaches/migraines
- ➤ Clenched teeth – jutting jaw
- ➤ Clenched fists – gripped thumb
- ➤ Coiled legs – arms folded
- ➤ Worry lines on forehead
- ➤ Foot/toe or hand/finger tapping – never physically still
- ➤ Nail biting and hair twirling
- ➤ Hair loss
- ➤ Shaky hands
- ➤ Grinding teeth
- ➤ Nervous voice
- ➤ Breathing problems
- ➤ Fatigue or tiredness
- ➤ Eczema/psoriasis
- ➤ Susceptibility to minor health problems – colds, etc.
- ➤ Major health problems – heart disease, breakdown, ulcers, etc.
- ➤ Changes in bodily functions
- ➤ Bowel problems
- ➤ Insomnia
- ➤ Nausea
- ➤ Breathlessness without exertion
- ➤ Sexual problems
- ➤ Don't want to get up in the morning even after sleeping well
- ➤ Nightmares
- ➤ Stomach ulcers and acidity
- ➤ Stroke
- ➤ Sweating
- ➤ Joint and back problems

> **Exercise: Add your own specific physical changes.**
>
> ....
>
> ....
>
> ....

Emotional changes

➤ Feeling tense, angry and/or impatient with anyone for anything

➤ Feel ready to burst into tears and emotionally on edge

➤ Panic attacks in non-threatening situations

➤ Fear or feeling threatened for no good reason

➤ Feeling guilty and apologising for everything

➤ Feel everyone is out to get you – persecution complex

➤ Feel powerless, overpowered or overwhelmed

➤ Obsessions and addictions

➤ Depressed

Exercise: Add your own specific emotional changes.

Fight, flight or freeze?

What is 'fight, flight or freeze'?

Any book you read about stress will refer to 'fight or flight' or 'fight, flight or freeze' as a survival mechanism that prepares you to either fight for survival or run away when you're threatened.

It's your body's automatic response to danger – a series of dramatic physical changes designed to give you a burst of energy and strength. Once the danger is over, systems return to normal and you become physiologically relaxed again.

The Physiological Changes

When your body goes into the fight or flight state the following changes happen automatically: (Valerie J Sutherland and Cary L Cooper)

Heart: Your heart begins to beat faster and harder to pump blood containing oxygen and sugar to your major muscles to use for energy. You may feel your heart beating as you breathe more rapidly.

Lungs: Your breathing rate increases and your airways dilate. More oxygen enters your blood.

Ears: Your hearing, indeed all of your senses become more acute.

Eyes: Your pupils dilate to help you see better. Your peripheral vision is also heightened.

Brain: Mental activity and alertness increase for quick decision making.

Blood: Your blood flow to muscles will increase to prepare for flight. The blood will thicken to increase the availability of clotting factors and immune system cells in case of an injury.

Legs and arms: Sugars and fats are converted for use as energy and sent to your major muscles to help you to fight or run away.

Skin and sweat glands: Sweating increases. Hands and feet often feel cold as blood supplies are diverted to the brain and muscles. Hairs stand on end as we experience goose pimples. Skin can turn pale.

Salivary glands: There is a decreased flow of saliva. Your mouth can feel dry.

Gut muscles: Gut activity slows as blood supply is reduced. This can affect digestion and cause digestion issues.

Spleen: Contracts and empties red blood cells into the circulation.

Kidneys: Reduced urine formation.

Liver and fat tissue: Glucose and fats mobilised for energy to fuel the muscles.

These responses are regulated by the sympathetic nervous system and by hormones such as cortisol, adrenaline and noradrenalin which are released into the blood stream.

The process occurs very quickly and is not a conscious decision.

Physical threats

An ancient response to physical threats, fight or flight would have been very valuable to our prehistoric ancestors, as they faced physical danger many times throughout their short lives. (Jeff Davidson, 1999)

It still helps to protect us by heightening awareness and helping us deal with emergencies. For example it enables us to react very quickly and slam on the brakes when someone runs in front of the car. However, once the acute stress is over, our bodies quickly return to normal.

The problem is that these days most of us are more likely to have to cope with psychological threats and stressors, like pressure of deadlines, traffic queues, delays, disagreements at work and office politics. They're not situations where physical aggression or running away are the best answers – and yet our bodies react as if we're facing physical danger: with the fight or flight response.

Psychological threats

Our psychological threats and stressors are different for each of us, based on our experiences, coping mechanisms, how we view life, our rules and beliefs, values, boundaries and measures of what's too much and out of balance.

As modern life gets more pressured and complex, we add more and more psychological triggers to the list.

Constant threats – Chronic stress

With the fight or flight physical changes, you're wired for action.
You're ready to face the threats and do your best.

Things that can trigger the fight or flight response.
(Dennis Greenberger and Christine A Padessky, 1995).

Feeling threatened by:

Being asked to do things you don't want to do

Being asked to do things you can't do

➢ Working overtime
➢ Exams
➢ Unwanted change

Perceived threats or fears:
➢ Not being accepted
➢ Being embarrassed
➢ Being laughed at
➢ Being rejected

Some psychological threats and stressors:
➢ Pressures of deadlines
➢ Traffic queues
➢ Disagreements at work
➢ Office politics

We can be in and out of this fight or flight state many times
throughout a day. (Jeff Davidson, 1999) This means we can be 'wired
up' almost constantly – with dangerous consequences for our health.

The worst problem is the response to psychological triggers, to simple, not truly life-threatening events. Often, there's no defined enemy to fight or run away from, and yet your body is on the alert and keyed-up for action. It's left with the hormones and chemicals that would have otherwise been quickly removed or used up during the physical reaction it expected. (Nancy Slessenger)

The fats released that are not used are likely to be restored in the lining of the arteries. This can increase blood pressure, making the heart work harder to pump blood around the body through these smaller capillary openings. (Valerie J Sutherland and Cary L Cooper, 2000)

As your body works hard to prepare for physical activity it releases stored sugars, glucose, glycogen, nutrients and fats required for the process. This not only drains your body, it also depletes vital stores and takes further energy to release or restore anything converted which hasn't been used.

Ineffective digestive and bowel functionality can also lead to irritable bowel syndrome (IBS), constipation, diarrhoea, indigestion and stomach ulcers which are all commonly related to stress.

As if this weren't enough, stress inhibits the immune system, making you more vulnerable to colds, flu, fatigue and infections.

Adrenal stress and fatigue

The adrenal glands are small walnut-sized glands on top of each kidney. They manufacture and excrete hormones that affect every tissue, organ and gland in your body. They also help your body cope with stress.

The outer adrenal cortex controls essential metabolic processes.

It secretes about 30 steroidal hormones, including:
➢ Cortisol – regulates carbohydrate, protein, and fat metabolism
➢ Aldosterone – regulates water and salt balance in the body
➢ Steroid hormones that counteract inflammation and allergies.

The inner adrenal medulla releases:
➢ Adrenaline – affects blood pressure, heart rate and sweating
➢ Noradrenaline – helps regulate many of the processes influenced by adrenaline

If you're constantly in a state of stress, your adrenal glands become fatigued and that can badly affect your health.

Signs of Adrenal Fatigue

(Robert O Young PhD and Shelly Redford Young, 2005)

➢ You might find it hard to get up in the morning

➢ Takes longer to complete everyday and work tasks

➢ Forgetful and unable to concentrate

➢ Need tea, coffee and other stimulants to get you through the day

➢ Loss of sex drive

➢ Feeling tired and lacking in energy even after lots of sleep

➢ Poor immune system

➢ Feel more energetic around lunchtime

➢ Anxious, irritable and impatient

➢ Crave salt and salty foods

Dealing with adrenal stress

Adrenal stress is the result of being in a constant state of fight or flight from feeling physically or psychologically threatened.

This causes over activation of the adrenal glands and nervous system. It also causes an increase in heart rate and blood pressure. Due to the increased levels of cortisol in the bloodstream, your immune system and digestive system are suppressed.

There are a number of simple lifestyle changes you can make to treat adrenal fatigue (Vicky Wade):

✓ laugh more often

✓ take small breaks and lie down

✓ increase relaxation

✓ eat regular meals

✓ exercise (avoiding any highly competitive events)

✓ go to bed early

✓ sleep at least 8 hours

It's also advised to make specific changes to your diet. We cover eating and stress in more detail in session 5, but very briefly, a good diet for treating adrenal fatigue includes unrefined carbohydrates (whole grains) with protein and oils (nuts and seeds) at most meals – olive, walnut, fibre, flax and high-quality fish oil.

When they're stressed, most people reach for certain foods or drugs to help raise energy levels. These are often the foods or chemicals to be avoided and only serve to make things worse.

Avoid during this time:

- ✗ Sugars
- ✗ Caffeine
- ✗ Alcohol
- ✗ Smoking
- ✗ Carbonated drinks
- ✗ Processed foods
- ✗ Saturated fats
- ✗ Red meats
- ✗ Excessive animal protein and dairy.

Foods that will help at this time:

- ✓ Fruits
- ✓ Water
- ✓ Green leafy vegetables
- ✓ Salads
- ✓ Good fats, such as omega 3 oils
- ✓ Fish
- ✓ Whole grains.

Stress awareness and evaluations

The stress curve in session 2 will give you a good feel for your stress levels and how they're affecting your performance. Now we're going to look at things in a bit more detail.

Do you cope well with stress?:

Reveals how effective your coping strategies are and what you need to do to improve them.

Personality types A and B in relation to work:

Shows how much your behaviour is like A or B types at work.

Do you cope well with stress?

Choose TRUE or FALSE the following statements:

1	Too little stress can be as bad as too much.	❑ True	❑ False
2	I ensure I regularly eat a balanced healthy diet.	❑ True	❑ False
3	I play a sport at least once a week.	❑ True	❑ False
4	I have control over what happens to me and my life.	❑ True	❑ False
5	I find it easier to face difficulties than to avoid them.	❑ True	❑ False
6	I hardly ever drink alcohol or don't drink at all.	❑ True	❑ False
7	I generally manage my time well.	❑ True	❑ False
8	We all need some level of stress to function properly.	❑ True	❑ False
9	I'm always prepared to give my opinion on something.	❑ True	❑ False
10	I know what is important to me in my life.	❑ True	❑ False
11	My plans often work out, but if not I have a plan B.	❑ True	❑ False
12	I get good ideas and action them ensuring they happen.	❑ True	❑ False
13	I am able to ask for help when I need it.	❑ True	❑ False
14	I take time to relax at least once per week.	❑ True	❑ False
15	I avoid words like should/ought and must.	❑ True	❑ False
16	I am in good health and happy with myself.	❑ True	❑ False
17	I remember to breathe properly during times of stress.	❑ True	❑ False
18	I don't let fear of failure hold me back.	❑ True	❑ False
19	I expand my comfort zone regularly by doing new things.	❑ True	❑ False
20	The purpose of life is to be happy.	❑ True	❑ False
21	I have goals and dreams.	❑ True	❑ False
22	I believe that anything is possible.	❑ True	❑ False
23	I always use the stairs instead of a lift.	❑ True	❑ False
24	I eat regular meals and healthy snacks.	❑ True	❑ False
25	I understand sometimes life can be challenging.	❑ True	❑ False

26	I take supplements during times of stress.	❏ True	❏ False
27	When I'm angry I say so and find a rational solution.	❏ True	❏ False
28	Some people can cope with more stress than others.	❏ True	❏ False
29	I walk as often as I can.	❏ True	❏ False
30	We can train ourselves to cope with more stress.	❏ True	❏ False
31	I do regular exercise.	❏ True	❏ False
32	I don't drink more than one cup of tea/coffee per day.	❏ True	❏ False
33	I know I won't always be liked by everyone and that's okay.	❏ True	❏ False
34	I find it easy to sleep and have a good and regular sleep pattern.	❏ True	❏ False
35	I don't feel the need to be perfect at everything I do.	❏ True	❏ False
36	When things go wrong I consider what else I can do to resolve the situation.	❏ True	❏ False
37	I can start conversations with strangers.	❏ True	❏ False
38	I find saying 'thank you' easy when given a compliment.	❏ True	❏ False
39	I can express my feelings to others.	❏ True	❏ False
40	I can give compliments without feeling embarrassed.	❏ True	❏ False
41	I am generally a positive thinker.	❏ True	❏ False
42	I can say no and not feel guilty.	❏ True	❏ False
43	I think it is more important to make a decision than make none at all.	❏ True	❏ False
44	I run/walk/jog at least one mile three times a week.	❏ True	❏ False
45	I feel it's up to me to make things happen.	❏ True	❏ False
46	I drink around two litres of water per day.	❏ True	❏ False
47	I am good at thinking of alternative solutions.	❏ True	❏ False
48	I weigh up the advantages/disadvantages of choices.	❏ True	❏ False
49	I take responsibility for outcomes of my choices.	❏ True	❏ False
50	I can always find time for myself as well as others.	❏ True	❏ False

51	I have a good work-life balance and maintain it.	❏ True	❏ False
52	I believe in being organised.	❏ True	❏ False
53	I enjoy receiving compliments.	❏ True	❏ False
54	I read inspiring books.	❏ True	❏ False
55	We all need some stress, stress can be good.	❏ True	❏ False
56	I do not smoke.	❏ True	❏ False
57	I consider many ways to view an issue or problem.	❏ True	❏ False
58	I challenge my negative thoughts.	❏ True	❏ False
59	Stress can be a great motivator.	❏ True	❏ False
60	Stress can lead to serious illnesses if not managed.	❏ True	❏ False
	Total		

Score Evaluation

Score 1 point for every TRUE you chose.

Score 45 to 60:

You are very skilled at managing stress and pressure. You are
unlikely to suffer with stress related fatigue or illness if you
continue to manage your stress in this way. You are looking
after your physical and mental health by exercising regularly and
keeping a positive outlook therefore looking after your body
and mind which will keep you strong during times of stress. You
understand the need for managing stress and regularly practise
techniques and strategies to maintain a healthy life balance.
Remember to maintain this during any times of prolonged stress
to ensure you keep a healthy balance.

Score 30 to 45:

You have some good skills and practise coping techniques, most of the time, but perhaps don't fully apply them under times of intense or prolonged stress. Ensure you use more stress management strategies and techniques when pressure is exceptionally high or you may be prone to slipping into the stress trap. You need to go back to what you know and what works for you and remember to practise the basics so they become a habit and automatic, whatever the level of stress. Focus on building health and strength for your body as well as for your mind.

Score 15 to 30:

You probably know what you're supposed to be doing and have some good coping skills yet you don't always apply them. You may need to eat more healthily and exercise more plus include some good stress management strategies and relaxation into your life or you may be prone to stress, fatigue and illness. When stress occurs in your life you may not currently be as well equipped as other people to deal with it. You need to revise your strategies and implement more techniques or you may suffer unnecessary stress.

Score 0 to 15:

You do not cope with stress well and do not follow or even know many stress management strategies. It is possible you do not understand the benefit of good physical health, hydration and nutrition as great stress busters. You need to make some rapid changes to ensure you don't become stressed or suffer from any of the stress symptoms.

Personality types A or B in relation to work

Answer YES or NO to the following questions:

1	Are you nearly always punctual for appointments?	❑ Yes	❑ No
2	Do you communicate better with your co-workers than with your partner or friends?	❑ Yes	❑ No
3	Are you better able to relax on Saturday mornings than on Sunday evenings?	❑ Yes	❑ No
4	Are you more comfortable when you are idle than productive?	❑ Yes	❑ No
5	Do you carefully organise your hobbies?	❑ Yes	❑ No
6	Are you usually annoyed when kept waiting?	❑ Yes	❑ No
7	Are most of your recreational activities with work colleagues?	❑ Yes	❑ No
8	Do your partner or friends think of you as an easy-going person?	❑ Yes	❑ No
9	Do certain work colleagues make you feel aggressive?	❑ Yes	❑ No
10	In sport are you always trying to improve and win more often?	❑ Yes	❑ No
11	When under pressure, do you still take the extra time to make sure you have all the facts before making a decision?	❑ Yes	❑ No
12	Do you usually plan every step of the itinerary of a trip in advance and tend to become uncomfortable if plans have to change?	❑ Yes	❑ No
13	Do you enjoy small talk at a drinks party?	❑ Yes	❑ No
14	Do you tend to substitute your work for close personal relationships or could it be a way of avoiding them?	❑ Yes	❑ No
15	Are most of your friends in the same line of work?	❑ Yes	❑ No
16	Do you take work to bed with you when you are ill?	❑ Yes	❑ No
17	Is most of your reading work-related?	❑ Yes	❑ No
18	Do you work late more often than your peers?	❑ Yes	❑ No
19	Do you talk 'shop' over drinks on social occasions?	❑ Yes	❑ No
20	Do you become restless on holiday?	❑ Yes	❑ No

Evaluation of personality types and work

Q1: Yes = 1 No = 0
Q2: Yes = 1 No = 0
Q3: Yes = 1 No = 0
Q4: Yes = 0 No = 1
Q5: Yes = 1 No = 0
Q6: Yes = 1 No = 0
Q7: Yes = 1 No = 0
Q8: Yes = 0 No = 1
Q9: Yes = 1 No = 0
Q10: Yes = 1 No = 0
Q11: Yes = 1 No = 0
Q12: Yes = 1 No = 0
Q13: Yes = 0 No = 1
Q14: Yes = 1 No = 0
Q15: Yes = 1 No = 0
Q16: Yes = 1 No = 0
Q17: Yes = 1 No = 0
Q18: Yes = 1 No = 0
Q19: Yes = 1 No = 0
Q20: Yes = 1 No = 0

Score	Type
17 to 20	High A
12 to 16	A
10 to 11	A/B
0 to 9	B

Type B Characteristics

➢ Relaxed and thoughtful appearance
➢ Many interests outside work
➢ Tend to walk slowly
➢ Patient

Type A Characteristics

➢ Excessive competitiveness and search for advancement and achievement
➢ Accentuating various key words in ordinary speech without real need, and tending to utter the last few words of a sentence far more rapidly than the opening words
➢ Continual drive towards imprecise goals
➢ Preoccupation with deadlines
➢ Abhorrence of delays and postponements
➢ Mental alertness which tips over easily into aggression
➢ Constant impatience
➢ Feelings of guilt when relaxing

Type A Personality and stress

If you are a Type A personality then you could be causing yourself a lot of stress. You will need to identify some stress management tools which work well for you and be able to pro-actively manage your levels of stress on a daily basis.

Advice for Type A

➢ Understand your body and be able to spot the signs and signals of too much stress early on
➢ Do something about your stress, find strategies such as relaxation or breathing techniques that work well for you
➢ Eat healthily and avoid the trap of eating poorly and on the go
➢ Manage your time properly by learning time management skills
➢ Give yourself a break, don't be too hard on yourself as perfection doesn't exist
➢ Remember to exercise in moderation as it is also a great stress buster
➢ Take time out to go for a walk or read a book and learn the benefits of being still sometimes
➢ Learn to have patience in yourself and others
(Ivan Hatvany, 1996)

Personal Reflection – your starting point.

During my time training in this area I have come across many individuals who claim to either be incredibly stressed or totally unaffected by stress. When we look into it, the reality is often quite different and their judgement of themselves and others generally changes. During this session we have gone through many signs and symptoms of stress, so by now you should have a good idea of yourself and where you may have any 'danger spots'.

We have also worked through questionnaires which look at your coping mechanisms for stress and A and B type personalities in relation to your work. You should now have a thorough understanding of exactly where you are. It is now a good time to refer back to the stress curve diagram discussed in session 2 to ensure you are really where you think you are and where you would like to be. Wherever you are its okay. This is your starting point and wherever you are along the curve is recoverable even if you're at or near burn out (even though this may take longer and we recommend you seek professional help if this is the case).

Once you know your true starting point i.e. where you are today, you can start to do something about it. I find that most people don't really have a full understanding of this point. They feel that they are more or less stressed than they truly are which tends to mean they take no action or become negative, focusing on how others affect them, rather than taking personal responsibility for themselves. It is important to know exactly where you are so you can take the correct action which is why we have focused on assessing and discovering where you are throughout this section of the programme.

Up to this point we have talked about what stress is and the dangers of unresolved stress, now you have awareness of how it may be affecting you or could possibly affect you in the future. The rest of this programme focuses on what you can do and are going to do about it, to get yourself to the point of balance that's so important for our health and happiness.

You are now half way through the programme and should be starting to think about changes you would like to make to ensure you manage stress in a positive way. This will help you to change your life to the way you want it to be. Start to consider what changes you need to make and what changes you would like to make.

We will ensure we give you lots of tools and strategies, some of which you will like more than others but you may have other options you could explore too. Now is the time to start to consider your options. Your health and happiness are precious and it's your life so you need to take the actions as no-one else can or will do it for you. It's time to start contemplating and embracing change as we discussed in the personal reflection section of session 1 as change is central to managing stress and mapping your life out the way you want it to be.

Session 4

Thinking Strategies

"Begin challenging your own assumptions. Your assumptions are your windows on the world. Scrub them off every once in awhile, or the light won't come in." Alan Alda

Session 4:
Thinking Strategies

This session aims to help you explore the way we take in information from our environment and how we process it to make sense of our lives. It looks at how our different channels of perception (visual, auditory, and kinesthetic (movement and feelings)) work together to interpret reality; and how that reality is a very personal thing.

Objectives:

By the end of this session you will be able to:

✓ describe how your thinking influences your reality

✓ explain how compounding intensifies our experiences and why 'being positive' needs to be consistent across everything you do

✓ question your own thinking habits and identify negative thoughts

✓ use some simple but powerful techniques to change your negative thoughts and beliefs

Tools in this chapter:

✓ Thinking strategies – consider how different thinking styles affect our perception and reality of our levels of stress

✓ The brain process – understand how our brains work and how this compounds or alleviates our stress

✓ The compounding process – the conscious and unconscious steps we take to enhance or decrease our stress

✓ Filtering – how we receive and process information to come to a judgement or perception

✓ Positive and negative thinking – exercises to challenge both views and experience the effect it has on our physiology as well as our brain

✓ Are you a negative thinker? – a questionnaire to gain personal awareness

✓ Negative pattern breaker – a strategy to break negative thought and behaviour patterns

✓ Reframing beliefs – an exercise to change and reframe negative beliefs from session 1 into empowering and positive beliefs

Managing your Mental State

Did you know that you create your own reality?

That you have the power to be and feel whatever you wish?

If around 80 per cent or more of the stress you suffer is in your head, why not just change it and choose not to be stressed? Is it that simple? Is it possible to make changes and be in control?

Selective Perception

Every second we experience huge amounts of information but we only pay attention to a fraction. Our minds are constantly filtering the information they receive – ignoring what we don't need for the task at hand. If we didn't filter, we'd be overwhelmed by the sheer volume of stimulation. We wouldn't function.

Selective perception is **protective**. When we drive, for instance, it protects us from getting into an accident, as it stops us from noticing all the minor details around us that are not relevant to the task of driving the car. Selective perception helps concentration: for example, as I write this I'm filtering out all the 'normal' sounds – the hum of the computer, the planes overhead, people talking – so that I don't get distracted.

Psychologically, this selective perception explains how we create or justify our own reality. (M Sherif and H Cantril, 1945) We process what we choose to see and this is different for every person, depending on our 'filters of the world' – that is, what we choose to let in and choose to ignore or delete, generalise or even distort. We're constantly confirming our beliefs and interpretations. (Richard Petty et al 1981)

If we only see what we choose to notice, are we not choosing our reality and ignoring anything else we choose not to notice? Aren't we creating our own unique reality? If this is so, it makes sense that you can choose to change your reality.

'There are no facts, only interpretations.' Friedrich Nietzsche

Mind/body Connection –
The Brain's Processes

The most complex organ in your body, your brain is made up of around one hundred billion nerve cells, or neurons. Each neuron can connect with thousands of others, and millions of new connections are constantly being made and broken throughout your life.

These neural networks are where thinking, learning and memory take place. We can create them; we can keep them; we can change them.

According to Eric Jensen (1998) 'What the human brain does best is learn. Learning changes the brain because it can rewire itself with each new stimulation, experience, and behaviour.'

Nerve cells that fire together wire together; so if you practise something over and over again the neurons involved form a long-term relationship. We also know that nerve cells that don't fire together no longer wire together. They lose their long-term relationship; so every time we interrupt a thought process, the neurons involved in that neural network break links and form other relationships in other circuits.

We all see the world differently because we've all experienced it differently. So one person might associate love with pain and suffering, whereas someone else links it to joy and laughter. Some of us see things positively, some negatively.

But the point is, whether they're positive or negative, we can change our thoughts, habits and beliefs.

85

How you see the world, your thoughts, language patterns (the regular words you use), beliefs, mantras, affirmations, incantations (such as 'I'm not too bad' versus 'I'm good, thanks') can all be used to reinforce or destroy neural circuits.

If you've formed negative emotions and patterns, then feeding them every day will only serve to reinforce them. Changing thoughts and language patterns – that is, breaking the patterns – will help to destroy old connections and create new associations, forming new emotional links and feelings.

Changing the way you think changes your experiences and reality.

What reality are you going to choose?

Consider the following:

➢ The brain doesn't know the difference between something you actually do or did and something you imagine or imagined.

➢ An experience is stored as a memory. You store that memory in a way that allows you to feel how you want when you think of it.

➢ Every time you recall a memory it changes slightly and you recall it differently. Therefore you can make the feeling feel more intense whether it's good or bad.

➢ What we think is how we are.

➢ Words sculpt our inner world and subsequently shape our outer world.

(Sue Knight, 2002)

'Words as I speak or write them, make a path on which I walk.'
Diane Glancy

Compounding and Filtering

- ➢ What I think
- ➢ What I say
- ➢ What I write/text/email
- ➢ How my physiology is

... IS HOW IT WILL BE!!!

Remember, we create our own reality.

Words and images sculpt our inner world and subsequently shape our outer world. What we think and then say to ourselves (our inner dialogue) has an influence on what we see, hear and feel. Similarly our spoken words not only influence us but also the people who are listening. In other words, the meaning of our communication is, indeed, its effect. (Richard Bandler and John Grinder, 1975/76)

Have you ever heard of compounding? It's where small changes add together to make a big difference. If you think of a chess board and put one grain of rice in the first square, two in the second, four in the third, eight in the fourth, sixteen in the fifth etc., then did you know by the time you get to the thirty third square it would have more grains of rice than people on the Earth and by the sixty fourth square you'd have nine followed by eighteen zeros grains of rice just on that square?

This same principle is applied in the brain when you compound a person's thinking process with their spoken word, written word and their physiology – these all reinforce the processes that occur in the brain so that the understanding of a situation is more than the sum of the parts.

The compounding process

Individually, each of these has a powerful effect on our reality:

➤ Thoughts

➤ Spoken words

➤ Written words

➤ Physiology

Together, they compound to create our reality, reinforcing the effect.

Thoughts

Our thoughts are like PC software, programming the brain with what we choose to see, feel and focus on, our rules and beliefs and filters. The neural networks that we form become reinforced by cells constantly firing together. These become the associations we have between what we perceive in the external world and our feelings and emotions.

Language

Hearing our own voice results in more programming of our PC/brain. We hear our own voice and therefore don't question it. Worse still, others may agree with us, and that further reinforces the statement and its reality – 'It's going to be a stressful afternoon I can feel it!' responded to with, 'I know what you mean. I can feel it too!'

Try saying 'I'm great, thank you' instead of 'I'm not too bad'. Which would you rather feel?

Or try saying 'I could do with some more energy right now', rather than 'I'm really tired'.

Can you see/feel the difference?

Written word/text/email

Things seem to become more real when they're written down. The effect is even more potent if we're looking at our own handwriting. Just as we recognise our own voice without question, so we respond to our own handwriting, further programming the belief. This can also be reinforced by the letter/text/email that we receive in reply.

Physiology

Try for a moment to adopt the physiology of a depressed person, looking down, shoulders hunched, downward slope of your whole body, face expressionless or sad. Try to think of something really sad and get into the feeling as an actor would. When you have the body language and feeling, freeze and don't move. Now think of how excited and ecstatic you would feel if you had just won the lottery and were about to tell your best friend, but ensure you don't move at all.

Now adopt the stance and body language of the person who has just won the lottery and is about to tell their best friend. Stand tall with a huge smile on your face. Freeze when you are in the moment. Again don't move a muscle and now think of being sad or depressed.

What did you notice? Did you notice that when you were acting depressed and thought happy thoughts you wanted to move your body upward and smile? Did you also notice that when you were feeling happy and I asked you to feel depressed that you wanted to move your body downwards and stop smiling or frown?

The mind and body are connected and your body language communicates messages to your brain.

In very simple terms, to your brain, a smile = happy and a frown or sulk = sad. You can't frown and feel happy nor can you smile and truly feel sad, as you've just demonstrated. Your body needs to adjust to make the correct match.

Next time you're feeling something negative and want to change it to be happy, try smiling, even if it's not true (you can fake it until you make it!). It will have the same effect as the process we just demonstrated and shift the way you feel.

> Changing how you stand, how you hold your body and your facial expressions makes a massive difference to how you feel. Think about it – have you ever felt sad when you've been dancing or laughing?

When people are stressed they tend to hold their body rigid and hunch their shoulders, maybe clench their jaw, frown, screw up their hands into fists and sit, or walk in a rushed or intense way. Notice what you do and how you can make changes to send messages of calm, contentment, relaxation and control to your brain helping to shift you out of that negative state.

To sum up: You will change how you feel and how your day/reality is likely to be when you challenge and change:

- ✓ your thought processes
- ✓ your spoken language
- ✓ your written word
- ✓ or your body language

Changing just one of these will have a great effect.

Changing all will have a compounding effect which can bring about massive change.

> It may be a little strange a first, but with practise you'll soon be able to do this naturally, at will.

Be aware of your thoughts, the language you use and the way you appear to others. They all have a massive impact on you and on how others treat you.

Remember, you have a choice and you can change or adapt anything you choose. It may not always be a simple choice and it may take a while to find a suitable solution, but there is always is a choice and solution if you look hard enough.

Filtering – What goes in affects what comes out

Imagine your brain is like a computer programmed by what you think, what you say, your physiology, the people around you, the things you read and listen to.

What goes in is what comes out. So ...

➢ If your selective perception filter is negative and you only run negative software, you'll only ever get negative results.

➢ If your selective perception filter is positive and you run positive software, you'll get positive results.

It's a self-fulfilling prophecy.

Are you a negative-filter or a positive-filter type person?

Negative-filter person with compounding

Here's an example of how a negative person might experience a day:

Morning alarm clock goes off and they wake up. Before they open their eyes they start to think:

'It can't be time to get up – I'm so tired. I can't believe it's not the weekend yet. The week has dragged and it's been a real pain. I'm so stressed out all the time! I wish I didn't have to work there. I can hear it's raining again. I'll just press the snooze button and then I'll get up.'

When they've got up and are getting ready, they continue to think or speak to people in the house:

'Now I'm late. I shouldn't have had a snooze. The kids are driving me mad already and I've no time for breakfast as the traffic will be bad and I know it will be worse today. Why does it always rain in the UK? I hate living here!'

Arriving at work, they speak to colleagues and send a text and email to other colleagues reinforcing what they're saying about their day so far. Their physiology is also apparent as they're stomping around the office and grimacing at people.

A colleague smiles and says 'Good Morning! How are you today?'

'Is it? I'm not too bad, I guess. Stressed out as usual and looking forward to the end of the week, to get out of here! What time is the meeting? Bet it's going to be really boring and they'll be asking us to perform miracles as usual! Their attitudes are so bad, they really annoy me!'

What kind of reality is this person creating?

Do you think they realise they have a negative attitude?

Do you think they're ensuring these things happen?

Are they creating their own stress?

What goes through your mind daily as you wake up?

What kind of day and reality are you programming?

Are you creating unnecessary stress?

Exercise: How do YOU compound and filter?

What do you generally say to people when they ask how you are?

....

....

....

....

....

What could you say instead?

....

....

....

....

....

Are the people you choose to be around generally very positive or negative in their views?

....

....

....

....

....

Are your emails/text generally positive or negative?

....
....
....
....
....

Do you normally smile, frown or ignore eye contact with people?

....
....
....
....
....

If someone were to look at you and your facial expression (generally) what mood would they guess you were in?

....
....
....
....
....

Positive Thinking

Positive versus negative thinking

Most of us have heard about and can appreciate the value of positive thinking, and many of us have heard great stories about how people have used positive thinking to turn around huge problems in their lives, turning what some would see as failures into huge successes. Others may have even cured themselves of various illnesses including cancer with the power of positive thinking and positive beliefs.

We've all heard the old saying 'is the glass half-full or half-empty' meaning that you can view life and situations in two ways and that one will help (positive) and the other hinder.

So, what would happen if you focused on positive thoughts and really made the effort to remain totally positive (glass half-full) when trying to solve an issue?

Would it help you come up with workable solutions?

Would it feel different from looking at the problem negatively?

Exercise: Try this experiment:

Write a current issue or problem you have (choose a small one to start with!).

....

....

....

WARNING! Your solutions might need time to work out, and you might not be able to solve the problem straight away – but don't be put off. Think hard and come up with three solutions. **STAY POSITIVE** and don't let any negative thinking creep in to say you can't do it – maybe you can't do it right now but you will be able to do it or alter it somehow if you look and think hard enough.

Now being totally POSITIVE consider how you could look at this problem differently.

....

....

....

Write down why you need to solve this problem and what you'll gain from it.

....

....

....

Write down three things you could do to solve it. (Include resources you could acquire and people who could help you – you don't have to do it on your own!)

....

....

....

Now look at the problem, at the reason you wanted to solve it, the benefit of solving it and the list of suggestions you have.

Write down honestly how you feel right now.

....

....

....

Now being totally NEGATIVE consider how you can't solve this problem.

Write down why you can't and won't solve this problem and what pain and loss it causes you by not solving it.

....
....
....

Write down three reasons why you cannot solve it.

....
....
....

Now look at the problem, at the pain and loss of having it and the list of reasons you have that you can't solve it.

Write down honestly how you feel right now.

....
....
....

Did you feel sad, hopeless, in pain, suffering, stuck, lost, depressed, down, angry, resentful, bitter or another negative emotion at the end of the NEGATIVE thoughts?

Did you feel hopeful, thoughtful, challenged, motivated, calmer, happier, determined or another positive emotion at the end of writing the **POSITIVE** thoughts?

You should have noticed a distinct difference in your physiology, how you felt emotionally and what you thought for each one.

Which task was easier?
The chances are that the easier task reflects your habitual thinking style.

Positive thinking makes a real and practical difference to problem-solving because:

✓ It puts you in a 'can-do' frame of mind

✓ It encourages you to believe that there are solutions – you've just got to find them

✓ It stops you sabotaging yourself

✓ It gives you more possibilities to choose from

✓ It helps you think more clearly

✓ It gives you the courage to try new ideas

Negative thinking makes the whole process as hard as can be and encourages us to give up as soon as we hit an objection, however small.

BUT . . .

Negative thinking patterns are only habits we've built up over the years and it is possible to change.

As we've already discussed during compounding and filtering – we create our own reality. Choose a good one!!!

Are you a negative thinker?

The first step is to be aware of your thoughts so you can identify the kind of things you say to yourself. This may be difficult at first, but with practise you will soon become skilled at noticing the negative things you say to yourself (your inner dialogue).

> Some of the following questions can help you to identify whether your thoughts are negative and assist you in challenging them.

- ❑ Do I call myself negative names?
- ❑ Do I predict the future negatively?
- ❑ Do I compare myself negatively to others?
- ❑ Do I make things out to be worse than they really are?
- ❑ Do I use words like never, should, ought, must, always, every?
- ❑ Do I pretend or make assumptions that I can read other people's minds by thinking this?
- ❑ Do I concentrate on my weaknesses and forget my strengths?
- ❑ Do I blame myself for something that is not my fault?
- ❑ Do I expect myself to be perfect?
- ❑ What is the evidence for or against the truth of your thought?
- ❑ What would other people think in a similar situation?
- ❑ Does this thought help me to get what I want?
- ❑ How would I see someone else in my situation?
- ❑ How would I have seen this situation before I became stressed about it?

Negative-pattern breaker

How to change being negative about yourself and others.

To change any pattern you just need practice or repetition – after all that is how you formed your negative patterns in the first place.

1. Every time you think about something negative ask yourself why you are thinking it and what benefit it has to you or others.
2. Change your thought to something that is positive. That will have benefit or good feelings towards yourself or others – you can find the good in any situation.
3. Write down or repeat that new thought a few times in your head and note how it feels different from the old thought.
4. Always correct and change your negative thoughts.
5. Soon you will think of the positives naturally and change your thought patterns.
6. Do not voice negative thoughts, only speak of the positive ones (do not validate them).
7. Try noting down every time you have a negative thought and assess if they are about the same subject. You will also notice how often you think these thoughts which for some can be a shock.

Sometimes positive thinking alone isn't all that's required to change limiting beliefs, problems and issues in life and manage stress more effectively.

It's important to acknowledge feelings and be true to yourself about negative emotions, as you feel them for a reason. It's also important to understand why the emotion is there and then look at the ways to change it. Cognitive therapy suggests (Rian McMullin) that people should consider many different angles on a possible problem. Looking at the situation from many different sides, positive, negative and neutral can lead to new conclusions and solutions (Dennis Greenberger and Christine Padessky).

Positive thinking coupled with developing strategies and taking action can bring about profound changes.

Positive beliefs

✓ The only person in the world we can change is ourselves

✓ Our influence comes from within ourselves

✓ If we do what we have always done we will get what we have always got

✓ Each person is unique and it is important to respect that difference

✓ Everyone makes the best choice available to them at the time they make it

✓ We have all the resources we will ever need within ourselves right now

✓ Mind and body are one and each influences the state of each other

✓ There is a solution to every problem

✓ The person with the most flexibility of thinking and behaviour has the most chance of succeeding

✓ There is no failure, only feedback and learning

✓ The significance of our communication is not its intention but its affect

---

Exercise: Add 3 of your own or choose 3 from the list that you will adopt as your own.

....

....

....

....

....

....

Reframing negative beliefs

You have the power to change, enhance, create and discard any beliefs that don't serve you.

Start by identifying the negative belief you want to change. Write it down (remember the power of the written word!) and then write down what you would like to believe instead.

Here's an example of what I mean:

Old belief: I need to do more.
New chosen belief: I am happy with what I do and know it's enough for me.

Old belief: I have to eat everything on my plate.
New chosen belief: I will eat until I feel full, and respect and value my body.

Old belief: It's selfish to take time out for me.
New chosen belief: It's important to take time to look after myself so I have energy for others.

Old belief: I mustn't fail.
New chosen belief: I am free and open to learning new things, discovering what works and what doesn't and taking my learning to a higher level.

Old belief: I have to control everything.
New chosen belief: I can only control myself. Sometimes, letting go allows me to grow and enjoy the freedom of trusting in the process.
Whatever happens, I will always be OK.

Make sure you list the new beliefs in a positive way, avoiding words like 'try', 'should', 'may' and so on, and negatives such as: 'I do not', 'will not', 'am not', 'used to be/do'.
Use words like: 'will', 'am already' and 'can'.

Exercise: reframing your old beliefs

Find your limiting beliefs from session 1. Transfer them to the old negative belief boxes in the chart.

Consider how you can change – 'reframe' or 'reword' – each one to become an

EMPOWERING POSITIVE BELIEF or STATEMENT. Remember, you don't have to believe the new belief right now, you just need to think about it and write it down then read it out to yourself (say it) and experience how it feels in your body and the difference you feel, where and how it feels different to the old belief.

Then, write the new beliefs in your diary or put them on a wall or somewhere you can read them and speak them out every day as affirmations, mantras or incantations.

Old belief	New POSITIVE belief

Personal reflection – creating your own reality, understanding perception

There is so much that we do not know about the human brain. However, we do know is that there is a mind – body connection which has been tested and demonstrated in many ways. We have looked at some examples of this during this session. There are many scientific and alternative theories that help to understand the human psychology and physiology of fight or flight – all focus at some point on how we automatically react or choose to react based on our perception of our reality.

If our own perception is our own reality, surely it would make sense to choose a good reality and concentrate on that? We have covered many areas now such as thinking patterns, thinking errors, compound thinking/communicating and negative versus positive thinking. Have you started to believe yet that we could choose our reality and therefore our levels of stress? This may seem a little alternative for some but the proof is in the pudding as they say, so why not give it a go? Focus on what you want for a change rather than what you do not want.

Do an experiment for yourself:
- ✓ Concentrate on being in control of your life
- ✓ Focus on all the good things
- ✓ Think about all the things you'd like to change becoming positive experiences
- ✓ Imagine interactions with challenging people becoming easy
- ✓ Believe that all the situations which caused you stress are now improving

At the very least for the time whilst you are doing this you will feel a lot calmer, happy and relaxed (great to do first thing in the morning as you wake and last thing at night just before you sleep). Another way to enhance this is to become grateful for all the things you have now and all the things you would like to have (imagine and feel as though you already have them). Gratitude is always the place I go to when I get stressed as it reminds you of how lucky you really are and puts everything into perspective – plus its really hard to feel negative or stressed when you're truly feeling grateful. If you practise this for two weeks continuously I guarantee you will surprise yourself with some profound positive results.

Coming back to how we perceive the world and information directed towards us, we can look at an NLP model called our 'Model of the World and Filtering'. This takes a look at how each person is unique and interprets things in their own way. When information or communication is directed at us we filter it and do one, all or a combination of the following three things – it is impossible for us to do none.

- ➢ Distort
- ➢ Delete
- ➢ Generalise

We have to do one or more of the three because of our beliefs and previous experiences. Most of the time it's done unconsciously. However, if we think about how we filter information presented to us we can become consciously aware of it and start to change how we view it. This will be assisted by working on changing negative beliefs and challenging your general view of the world especially if it seems quite negative.

We can delete information given to us. For example if someone says, 'Your presentation was excellent but the last slide had too much detail in it.', the person hearing it could delete the good feedback and just hear, 'Your last slide had too much detail in it.' They would delete the positive message and focus on the negative. Do you think this could cause them to feel stressed? It certainly could and that was not the correct message, they changed it themselves by filtering it and deleting some of the content.

People can also distort information, 'I can't make the appointment with you on Tuesday but I could go on Wednesday.' Someone who distorts information could hear something completely different and in their mind may interpret that message to be 'I don't want to go with you.' A very different message and one which could cause stress and conflict because of how it was distorted.

'Everyone thinks I'm too slow.' is something someone could say or think if they were generalising. It's a little like exaggerating, 'everyone' could be just one person many years ago who made a passing comment which the receiver distorted and generalised and then formed into a belief.

There are many ways to delete, distort and generalise and many examples, some of which I am sure you have already identified for yourself.

Recognising how you filter information and communication directed towards you is a great start in changing your existing filter patterns to a more positive outlook and ensuring you hear and interpret the real message. After all, you now know that whichever way you interpret information it will be your reality and the root of how you decide to react. Concentrate on how you communicate information and how you choose to receive and interpret communication from others.

Session 5

Health, Exercise and Relaxation

"The greatest wealth is health." Virgil

Session 5:
Health, Exercise and Relaxation

This session aims to help you to understand how stress affects health and the immune system, creating an environment of ill health and chronic fatigue. We saw the affects that the 'stress state' has on the body in session 3. We're now going to look at how to look after yourself to ensure the immune system is fully supported, to avoid illness during stressful times, improve memory and concentration which tend to be reduced during these times, and create and maintain higher levels of energy.

Objectives:

When you've practised the ideas in this chapter, you will be able to:

✓ describe a healthy, balanced eating plan and say why it's so important in the fight against stress

✓ make any necessary changes to your eating habits

✓ judge whether you're getting enough exercise to help combat stress

✓ judge whether you're getting enough effective relaxation to help combat stress

✓ work out what kinds of exercise and relaxation are right for you

Tools in this chapter:

✓ Healthy eating

✓ Hydration – understanding how crucial water is to being healthy and happy

✓ Relaxation – a full relaxation script you can record yourself or get someone to read to you

✓ Breathing exercises – six quick and easy breathing techniques to use any time, any place

✓ Neck exercise – a full neck exercise to help you to de-stress after a long day or journey

✓ Meditation – a meditation guide to use and adapt yourself

✓ Sleep – suggestions on how to get the most restorative sleep

The information in this session is based on the work of experts such as Dr Udo Erasmus, a leading expert on fats and how they help or harm the body; Dr Robert O Young, a nutritionist and microbiologist who focuses on the pH balance of the body; Dr F Batmangjelidj, an expert in hydration and the body's need for quality water; plus nutritionists and authors such as John Robbins, Patrick Holford and Lesley Kenton.

Why think about what you eat?

Our modern, busy lifestyles seem to have encouraged many of us to turn away from healthy wholesome food claiming we have no time, that we need convenient, quick ready-made food. The supermarkets and fast-food giants have significantly contributed to this way of living as they actively market the convenience foods and provide the intensely farmed and what some would describe as 'empty' foods.

As Gillian McKeith famously said: 'YOU ARE WHAT YOU EAT'

Poor eating, ill health and certain health-related diseases are on the increase. (Patrick Holford, 2002) Many studies have been conducted linking children's hyperactive and difficult behaviour to certain food groups and additives. Foods lacking in essential oils, vitamins and nutrients, full of hormones, pesticides, antibiotics, additives and flavourings are being widely consumed with varying short and long term side effects and consequences. Jamie Oliver (school dinners) and other health pioneers are proving over and over what a tremendous affect food can have on people's general health, weight, wellbeing, behaviour, intelligence and concentration.

> During times of prolonged stress, your body and immune system aren't able to function properly and they become weak. If you don't eat well to replenish energy, vitamins, nutrients, vital fats or oils and so on, your body is forced to use its emergency stores. When stores are low or depleted, your body becomes weak and susceptible to infections, illness and chronic fatigue.

Many people currently eat a poor diet that becomes worse under times of stress, as they eat when rushing around or skip meals, squeeze in quick meals which are often takeaway foods, fast-food or convenience ready-microwave meals. Under stress people often smoke more, drink more alcohol and caffeine, adding to the problem and stressing the body further.

The statistics surrounding today's diets (American studies) are alarming:

➢ It is estimated that 30% to 40% of cancers could be prevented with better diet

➢ Out of the top 10 causes of death, 8 are diet-related

➢ 20% of all boys and 30% of girls will be obese by 2020

➢ Type 2 diabetes and coronary heart disease are related to obesity

➢ 60% of all world deaths are related to poor diets, with people consuming high amounts of fat, salt and sugar

Healthy eating to combat stress

During times of stress your body can become fatigued. So it's important to make sure that your diet isn't making things worse. Are your foods adding to your stress? Or are they helping you to cope better with life's pressures?

To support your immune system, and keep strong, you need to get the balance right!

This first diagram shows how most people eat: lots of refined carbohydrates such as ready-meals and snacks packed full of additives and preservatives, very little fresh fruit and vegetables or even water. A person with these kinds of eating habits is not very fit, and is prone to illness and infections. Their immune system and body's defence are low and they don't cope with stress well.

This is not a healthy balance.

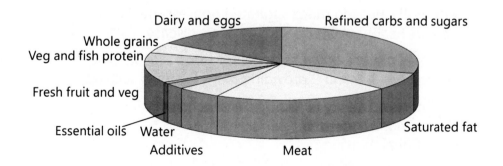

This second diagram, however, is a rough guide to the right balance for optimum health and strength to avoid stress and illness. It will make a massive difference to how you feel, think and look.

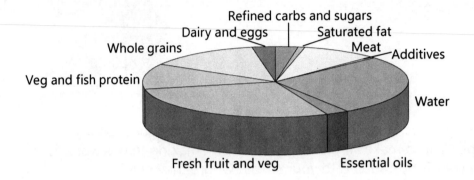

Water and breathing

Water and oxygen – hydration and correct breathing – are the first most important things for our bodies. It makes sense when you look at the body's priorities: we can't last more than a few minutes without oxygen, a few days without water, but we can last much longer without food.

Essential oils

Fats provide a lot of our energy. The body needs fat to function efficiently. But too much saturated non-essential fat can cause serious health problems such as heart disease.

Essential oils are called essential for good reason. Essential omega oils 3, 6 and 9 providing many benefits such as:

➢ improved clarity of thought and concentration
➢ hormone balancing
➢ rational thinking
➢ improved behaviour in children and prison inmates
➢ reduced risk of heart disease
➢ lowered cholesterol

➤ helping recovery from depression
➤ increased energy and performance
➤ improved quality of hair, skin and nails, including eczema and psoriasis.

The brain is 60 per cent fat (Udo Erasmus, 1993) so it makes sense that it requires healthy fats. Eating or supplementing with the full range of essential oils has many positive effects for the body generally as well as during times of prolonged stress and pressure.

Bad fats versus good fats

Most people wrongly believe that any fats make you fat. Too much saturated, non-essential fat can cause weight gain and can also cause serious health problems such as heart disease.

Essential fats, including polyunsaturated and monounsaturated fats are healthy fats, used by the cells in the body, helping in the metabolism and consumption of fats; that is, they help fats to be burned and used up rather than stored.

Non-essential fats are found in foods like:

➤ pastries
➤ fried foods
➤ meats
➤ cream
➤ cheese
➤ whole milk
➤ chocolate
➤ crisps
➤ cakes
➤ biscuits

Essential fats are found in foods like:

✓ nuts – natural, unsalted and unroasted
✓ seeds – pumpkin, sunflower, flax seeds etc
✓ oily fish – tuna, mackerel, trout, sardines, salmon
✓ avocados

Fresh fruit and vegetables

We all know the benefits of eating lots of fruit and vegetables – and there can't be many who haven't heard the famous 'minimum 5-a-day' rule . However, it's also important to consider where our fruit and veg come from and how they've been treated.

Green vegetables provide so many of the vitamins and nutrients the body needs. We need a minimum of five portions of fruit and vegetables per day. Vegetables are the best source as they're lower in sugar than fruit.

Most fruit and vegetables are imported and travel long distances to get to us. Once picked, they begin to lose their goodness; and the longer they're left uneaten, the more goodness they lose.

Also, the nutrient content of soil in some areas can be lacking leaving the produce low in nutrients. Herbicides and pesticides are widely used to grow and protect produce that we ingest.

The best source of fruit and vegetables are local farmers and markets. If you're able to buy organic produce, it will also be free of herbicides and pesticides and generally taste much better. There are lots of farmers' markets and box-delivery schemes where your weekly organic fruit and veg can be delivered directly to your door.

Vegetable and fish protein

Your body needs proteins for cell growth and repair.

Fruits and vegetables contain a certain amount of these proteins.

Good sources of plant proteins are peas, beans, grains and lentils. Some plant proteins don't contain all or enough essential amino acids, so vegetarians should try to eat a mixture of nuts, cereals or beans.

Fish is a healthy option and oily fish such as salmon, mackerel, tuna, trout and sardines are great choices as they're rich in the essential omega oils.

Meat

Meat eaten in moderation is fine. However, your body doesn't need a huge amount of protein and actually needs a lot less than you think. Eight per cent of your daily calorific intake is more than enough. In fact, just over four per cent would be sufficient. (Patrick Holford, 2002)

You can also get a lot of protein from vegetables, nuts and seeds. If you eat meat, try to find a local butcher or supplier who provides organic meat so you know where it comes from.

Whole grains

Whole grain means that all three parts of the grain are used.

➤ Bran – the coarse outer layer with the most fibre
➤ Endosperm – largest part of the kernel, with the most carbohydrate and protein
➤ Germ – the 'heart' of the grain, rich in B vitamins, healthy oils and minerals

Grains such as basmati rice, jasmine rice, buckwheat, kamut, amaranth, quinoa, spelt and millet are excellent for your body and health, as well as being high in protein and low in fat.

Carbohydrates

There are two types of carbohydrates: simple and complex. Both are found in either natural or refined forms.

Simple carbs or sugars:
➤ Natural sugars – in fruit and vegetables
➤ Refined sugars – in foods such as brown and white sugar, ready-made meals, chocolate and sweets, biscuits, cakes and pastries.

Complex carbs or starch:
➤ Natural complex carbs – slow-releasing energy foods such as bananas, brown rice, chick peas, beans and barley
➤ Refined carbs – in foods such as white bread, pizza, pastries, pasta, white rice and processed breakfast cereals.

Complex natural carbs are ideal as they release energy slowly. Anything that has been refined has been processed and has lost some of its fibre, vitamin and mineral content.

Dairy and eggs

Eggs and dairy products such as whole milk and cheese are also high in saturated fat. Some yoghurts are high in sugar or sweeteners. Lactose is the sugar found in milk and many people can not digest lactose.

Standard milk is highly processed and can contain hormones. Organic milk or better still oat, soya, rice and almond milks are now widely available. Be aware, some alternative milks are sweetened.

Try the alternatives to milk, yoghurts and cheese; or eat dairy in moderation.

Vitamins and minerals

Vitamins and minerals are essential nutrients that help the body function properly. There are official recommended daily intakes to help people avoid deficiency and stay healthy.

Vitamins come from many sources: Vitamin C from foods such as citrus fruits, tomatoes, melons, strawberries; Vitamin D from green vegetables, oily fish, milk, eggs; Vitamin B1 from foods such as liver, peas, potatoes, eggs and grains.

Minerals are as important to good health as vitamins and comprise about 20 chemical elements. Leafy vegetables and fish are good sources of minerals.

During times of stress, supplements can help support your immune system and provide much needed energy, vitamins, nutrients and minerals to keep your body strong to avoid illness.

Recommendations are:

➢ A good quality multi-vitamin and multi-mineral complex
➢ An antioxidant complex
➢ Supplement of Omega 3/6/9 oil if not present in the diet

Additional supplements may be required and you should consult your doctor or nutritionist to discover your exact needs. The British Nutrition Foundation www.nutrition.org.uk and Health Supplements Information Service www.hsis.org sites will be able to give you specific direction and recommendations.

Summary of healthy eating

The benefits of healthy eating are:

✓ Optimum health

✓ Strengthened immune system

✓ Achieving and maintaining natural body weight

✓ Obtaining an abundance of energy

✓ Increased concentration and mental clarity

✓ Stabilising hormones and mood swings.

Remember, during times of stress the general tendency is to skip meals or eat convenience or junk foods to save time, and to rely more heavily on stimulants and sugars for energy and comfort such as tea or coffee, alcohol, nicotine, fizzy caffeine drinks and chocolate. These foods stress the body further and they do not provide good nutrition. That means your body is working harder and is also using water to flush toxins out, causing further dehydration and depletion.

The recommended way of eating to combat stress, keep energy levels high, avoid illness and disease is to:

- ✓ Drink an average of two litres of quality water per day – eight to ten glasses to hydrate your body
- ✓ Reduce your meat intake and eat more fish and vegetable proteins
- ✓ Reduce or eliminate poisons and toxins such as sugar, coffee, alcohol, tobacco, chocolate and other stimulants relied on during times of stress
- ✓ Eat more raw vegetables and salads and fewer processed foods; approximately 70 per cent of your plate should be vegetables or salad
- ✓ Eat dairy products in moderation

Changing eating habits is not an overnight process. Small steps with changes made slowly and gradually will help you maintain these new conscious behaviours and transform them into long-lasting habits.

It's interesting to note that when you eat this way, your taste buds can change and cravings for the sugary or salty foods disappear. You may find you don't want what you would call 'treats' anymore as they no longer appeal to you and you can feel the difference they make to your body when you do eat them.

One step at a time

It's well worth making changes, even if you only take tiny steps, as small changes will have big effects for you.

You'll notice you have far more energy, feel amazing, sleep better, be more positive, achieve and maintain the ideal body size for you and avoid illness, especially during times of stress and pressure.

And finally ...

As we've seen, stress can have a massive impact on your body, resulting in various symptoms, illnesses and diseases. It's clear that correct nutrition via a healthy diet is crucial during these times. This helps to keep your immune and digestive systems strong enough to deal with the excess pressure placed upon them, so you don't fall prey to illnesses and viruses. The adrenal glands also need to be kept strong when fighting stress and aiding with recovery from illness.

Healthy eating and hydration are fundamental to good health and stress management, and can make a profound difference to how you and your body cope during stressful times.

Hydration

Water and correct hydration are incredibly important to our health and wellbeing; even mild dehydration can slow the metabolism by three per cent. Lack of hydration is the number one cause of daytime fatigue. Just a two per cent drop in water can cause fuzzy short-term memory, trouble with basic maths and difficulty in focusing on the computer screen or a printed page.

Stimulants such as tea, coffee and other caffeine drinks, and depressants such as alcohol, all dehydrate your body. Yet in times of stress, people tend to increase their consumption of them.

Most people know that the human body is about 50 per cent water by volume. The average adult male/female has approximately 40 litres of water in their body.

Recommendations

➤ Drink at least two litres of water a day. It's best sipped throughout the day as your body doesn't store water well.

➤ Start the day with a large glass of water as soon as you awake. We're the most dehydrated in the morning, so this is a good practice to get into.

➤ If you want to drink alcohol, fizzy drinks and caffeine, make sure you accompany them with a large glass of water.

Signs of dehydration

If you're dehydrated you could suffer from things like headaches, weight gain, allergies, high blood pressure, bloating and water retention. You may notice if you are dehydrated that your urine is yellow or smelly. Your urine should be clear unless it's first thing in the morning or you're taking any particular vitamins.

Top tips

If you have a headache, drink a large glass of water. If the headache is due to dehydration, it should be gone within twenty minutes.

If you're hungry between meals, you could actually be thirsty. So drink a glass of water and wait twenty minutes. If you're still hungry, then you really are!

And remember, if you're thirsty then you're already dehydrated – don't wait, keep sipping water throughout the day, every day.

Physical Exercise

Physical fitness improves your body's ability to cope with stress and releases tension.

Exercise needs to be regular. A good mix of aerobic exercise and resistance training will strengthen your body and immune system and avoid producing lactic acid which further stresses your body and causes the muscle pain that often reduces motivation.

Exercise is great for your body and your mind as it releases endorphins which make us feel good and focuses your mind away from worries and problems.

Exercise: Exercise audit

How much exercise do you currently do each week?

....

....

....

How much do you think you could be doing?

....

....

....

Are there opportunities for you to combine exercise with other activities, eg. walk the kids to school, climb the stairs at work?

....

....

Why do you exercise? Or why don't you currently exercise? What could motivate you to do more exercise?

....

....

What forms of exercise do you enjoy doing?

....

....

What exercise can you plan to do in the week ahead? (Start small if you currently do none.)

....

....

Optimum exercise and energy

A good combination would be a mix of aerobic and resistance training which will help burn excess fat and keep muscles strong and toned which, in turn, will burn more calories a day.

Try to avoid anaerobic exercise as your body burns carbohydrates and sugars rather than fats and has a by-product of producing lactic acid which stresses your body.

Even if you only start with a few minutes, you'll soon feel the difference.

Types of exercise

There are many different types of exercise for you to choose from. Whichever you choose make sure it is safe for you to do (consult your doctor to make sure) and that you will enjoy it. Exercise is about fun especially if you are using it as a stress buster and to motivate you to do more and continue to do it enjoying it is essential.

Here are some suggestions but there are many more things that you could consider:

- ✓ Dancing
- ✓ Walking
- ✓ Running
- ✓ Gardening
- ✓ Swimming
- ✓ Diving
- ✓ Skiing
- ✓ Step
- ✓ Aerobics
- ✓ Trampolining
- ✓ Skipping
- ✓ Weight training
- ✓ Yoga
- ✓ Pilates
- ✓ Sailing
- ✓ Team sports
- ✓ Surfing
- ✓ Cycling

ENJOY!

Relaxation and Meditation

Learning to Relax

Relaxing both body and mind is a very potent way of dealing with stress. However you choose to relax – whether it's playing golf, doing housework or jogging, having an aromatherapy massage or a hot bubble bath – it's important to plan and enjoy your relaxation time.

If you're looking for more focused relaxation, these are some of the more common techniques:

Yoga – various different types of yoga, focusing on toning and stretching the muscles, meditation, breathing and relaxation to focus the mind.

Pilates – focusing on the strength of the core body muscles for exercise, strength and relaxation via breathing techniques.

Aromatherapy – using essential oils with particular aromas to aid relaxation.

Flotation – floating in a water tank filled with a solution of mineral salts in a warm, dimly lit environment.

Indian Head Massage – using finger pressure and massage on certain areas of the head, neck and shoulders to relieve stress and tension.

Shiatsu Massage – performed fully clothed.

Hot Stone Therapy – hot stones used during the massage process.

Meditation – done in silence or with music, chanting or gongs to help focus and silence the mind.

> Whichever technique you practise remember, there is no one RIGHT way to practise. Explore the many approaches available and choose what works best for you.
>
> Don't force yourself. Allow the techniques to just happen, and observe the difference.

You need to schedule at least one hour of relaxation time every two weeks, and if you can allocate time more often, do so.

Relaxation really is as important as any of the other stress management techniques, including exercise and nutrition. It's not an indulgence.

Let's look at some simple – but effective – techniques you can do on your own. We'll start with the basics – getting your breathing right

How to Breathe Properly

Try these techniques a few times and see how they feel.

If at any time you feel faint or light headed please do stop and return to normal steady breathing.

Abdominal breathing

Abdominal breathing is the type of breathing you practise in yoga. Babies also breathe this way, as do you when you're asleep. It involves letting the air you breathe in push out your abdomen.

➢ Close your eyes and make yourself comfortable.
➢ Place both hands gently on your tummy so you can feel the rise and fall of the breath and ensure you're doing it correctly.
➢ If possible, breathe in and out through your nose. If you prefer, in through your nose and out through your mouth. If you have a cold you may need to breathe in and out through your mouth.
➢ Imagine you have a round balloon in your stomach you want to inflate. As you breathe in, imagine the air going down through your lungs and continuing into the stomach, fully inflating the balloon.
➢ As you exhale, the balloon deflates.

Rib cage breathing

This breathing technique is practised in pilates and also by ballet dancers.

➤ Close your eyes and make yourself comfortable.
➤ Place your hands on the lower side of your rib cage (both sides) so the fingers of each hand gently touch.
➤ Breathe in through your nose.
➤ This time, imagine you're filling a long narrow balloon which inflates out to both sides, gently pushing your rib cage out with it.
➤ Feel the air filling your lungs and your rib cage expanding outwards to the side.

You probably preferred one of the styles of breathing, so choose which suits you best and use it for the rest of these breathing techniques. You don't need to keep your hands in position unless it helps you to remember the technique.

Breathing Exercises

These exercises aim to switch off the adrenalin response, relax your body and calm your mind. A count is around a second.

> ### Exercise: Energy breathing
>
> This exercise brings more oxygen into your body and energises. If you do this and also have a big glass of water, you'll be able to avoid the afternoon energy slump and not need that cup of coffee.
>
> Do this exercise standing rather than sitting.
>
> ➤ Breathe in for 5 counts
> ➤ Hold for 20
> ➤ Breathe out for 10
> ➤ Repeat three times
>
> Good for creating energy – best done outside or by a window to get some cool fresh air. It is also good first thing in the morning or before an exercise workout.

Do the rest of these exercises sitting down.

Exercise: Square breathing

➢ Breathe in for 4 counts
➢ Hold for 4 counts
➢ Breathe out for 4 counts
➢ Hold for 4 counts
➢ Repeat for a few cycles

This is a yoga-style breathing technique. It focuses your mind on the breathing (and not the issue or problem), calms your body and reduces your heart rate. This is an excellent technique to do anywhere.

Exercise: Alternate nostrils

➢ Lightly hold your thumb to the side of one nostril and your index finger to the side of the other nostril
➢ Breathe in and out three times normally
➢ On the fourth inhalation, close the nostril with your thumb and breathe out through the open nostril
➢ Inhale through the open nostril
➢ Release your thumb and use your index finger to close the open nostril, releasing the other nostril
➢ Now breathe out through the open nostril
➢ Breathe in through the open nostril
➢ Then swap to the thumb to cover the open nostril and continue.
➢ Swap nostrils for rounds of inhalations and exhalations around eight times.

This is also a yoga breathing technique and has the same affects as the previous exercise. One to be done in private and not when you have a cold!

Exercise: Rapid exhalations

➢ Take a large breath in
➢ Then breathe out in quick short outbursts (about six to ten small quick bursts of air) from your nostrils so you can hear the exhalation
➢ You'll also feel this in your stomach as it contracts backwards and forwards.
➢ You'll find that you're breathing in as well as out, so you should be able to keep it going for at least six short bursts before you feel the need to breathe normally again
➢ Repeat three times.

Another yoga breathing technique, used to focus your mind, and good when used alongside other breathing techniques to prepare for meditation.

Exercise: Calming breath

➢ Breathe in for 7 counts
➢ Don't hold
➢ Breathe out for 9 counts

Commonly used for inducing calm during panic attacks. Can be used anywhere anytime. Especially good to use during arguments before you react or speak.

Exercise: Heartbeat breathing

As you inhale and exhale you're going to count the number of heartbeats you feel between each breath. Your aim is to increase your breathing cycle to take in more beats.

Use your index finger and the next finger to find your pulse in either your wrist or your neck. When you can feel the pulse, then start the exercise.

➢ Count the number of heartbeats as you inhale and exhale normally.
➢ When you've completed one breathing cycle and have a figure, complete a second cycle and try to increase the figure by one or two counts – you'll need to breathe in for longer, hold for longer or breathe out for longer to achieve this.
➢ Repeat for a third cycle and try to increase the figure by one.

A great exercise for creating calm and not being able to worry or be anxious about a problem – all your concentration is taken up with counting the beats.

As you continue with the exercise, it will get harder because your heart rate will begin to slow down as you relax, and you'll need to take deeper and longer breaths.

This is a Tai Chi breathing technique and experts can get twenty three beats per breath. You only need to be an expert in stress management breathing!

Tension release – Relaxation technique

1 Sit upright or lie down and get as comfortable as you can with your arms in an open posture, or on your thighs or chair arms. Uncross your legs and have your feet flat on the floor if sitting. Remove your shoes if you wish.

2 Close your eyes and begin to focus on your breath.

   Take three deep breaths from the abdomen and try to remain focused on the breath, allowing any thoughts to leave your mind.

   Zone out from any distractions or noise by bringing your focus and attention back to the breath.

3 Take your awareness to your feet and notice any tension present.

   Allow the tension to be released.

   Let the muscles in your feet go and let your feet feel heavy, as if they were sinking into the ground.

4 Now take your awareness to your ankles, calves, the front of your legs and all the way up to your knee sockets.

   Scan for any tension and let it go, allowing it to flow down your legs and out of the end of your toes.

   Remember to breathe, breathing in relaxation and allowing the breath to breathe out tension and anything you don't need.

5 Take your awareness to your upper legs and hips.

   Scan for any tension and let it go, allowing it to flow down your legs and out of the end of your toes.

6 Now move up to your stomach and lower back, up to your chest and upper back.

   Scan for any tension and let it go, allowing it to flow down your body, all the way down and out through the end of your toes.

   Breathing in deep relaxation and calm, and breathing out stress and tension.

7 Take your attention to your shoulders, upper arms, elbows and down through your lower arms.

   Allowing any tension you find to gently flow down your arms and be released through the ends of your fingers.

   Feeling more deeply relaxed and calm now.

8   Focus on the back of your neck, up the back of your head, top of your head to your forehead, eyebrows, eyes, behind your eyes, cheekbones, ears, tip of your nose, lips and chin

Allow any tension to flow away down and out of your body.

The breath bringing total calm and relaxation and removing any last bits of remaining tension from your whole body.

Your whole body now feels heavy and relaxed, fully supported by the chair or bed.

9   Imagine a beam of light entering the top of your head and gently scanning down your body for any tiny remnants of tension and dissolving them as it flows through.

It's a colour that you like or that means something to you.

When it reaches your feet, it changes to a colour of great healing and calm and starts an upward flow, filling your body, repairing and renewing anything that needs it as it goes along.

When it reaches the top of your head, the colour stays within the body.

10 There is nothing for you to do, only relax and focus on your breath.

Continue to breathe and focus on the colour you have chosen.

Relax here for a long as you like.

11 When you're ready to move, gently wiggle your fingers and toes and slowly open your eyes.

Allow yourself to come back to full consciousness slowly and have a good stretch before you stand up and continue with your day.

If you carry out this exercise regularly, you'll find it will refresh you and help you cope with the pressures and demands of life. The more you do it, the easier it will be and the quicker you'll be able to reach a deep level of relaxation.

Neck exercise

This exercise is fabulous, as it gently stretches all the muscles in the neck and shoulders where tension from stress tends to build up. If you have any neck or shoulder problems or injuries, please take care or skip this exercise.

Play some relaxing music whilst you do this, and take all the time you need to complete the exercise.

Make sure all movements are slow, deliberate and gentle. Do not rush or jolt any of the moves and if anything hurts, stop. It should feel good.

Exercise: Gentle neck movements

Do this exercise standing up or sitting down.

➢ Imagine you have a paintbrush at the end of your nose with your favourite colour paint on the end

➢ In front of you is a huge white canvas

➢ Paint the numbers 1 to 10 as big as you can on this canvas using all the movement and flow you need

➢ Focus on the music and on the breath, remembering to breathe properly and allowing the breath to release tension.

➢ Breathe in calm and relaxation.

Enjoy!

Meditation

Mediation is widely used for focusing the mind and creating a calm and stillness in the mind and body.

It can take practise to achieve, as thoughts of things to do, worries and concerns can pop into your mind. The aim is to silence your mind by focusing on the breath, and as thoughts come into your mind, releasing them and refocusing on the breath.

How to meditate:

Get yourself into a comfortable cross-legged seated position.

Or you could try sitting against the wall with your legs extended in front of you

➤ Place your arms loosely towards your knees and allow your hands to rest on your knees, palms up and open or touching the thumb and index finger together with the other fingers open and upwards.

➤ Close your eyes and begin to breathe using any of the relaxing breathing techniques listed previously.

➤ Focus on your breath and continue to breathe.

➤ Allow your breath to relax your body, and enjoy the effect as it quietens your mind.

After some practise, you'll be able to quieten your mind much more easily and also block out surrounding noises to create your own inner peaceful environment.

You can also use relaxing music, gongs and chimes to help you to meditate.

Stress and sleep

Everybody needs a different amount of sleep. For adults, the average is seven to eight hours a night, but some people only need four or five.

Worry and stress can deny us of valuable sleep and it is important during these times to get good quality sleep to provide the energy and clarity of thought to deal with the difficult issues or situations causing the stress.

Sleep deprivation causes:

- ✗ irrational thinking
- ✗ reduced memory
- ✗ impaired concentration
- ✗ weakened immune system
- ✗ lowering of body temperature.

Aids to good sleep:

- ✓ Take a hot relaxing bath before bedtime
- ✓ Keep to routines of sleep patterns; i.e. go to bed and get up at the same time each day to develop a specific pattern or routine
- ✓ Do breathing exercises to aid relaxation
- ✓ Avoid alcohol and caffeine before bed
- ✓ Don't drink too much fluid before bed
- ✓ Herbal teas such as camomile, valerian and passiflora are good to relax with
- ✓ Read something light
- ✓ Listen to relaxation CDs or calming music
- ✓ Listen to sleep/relaxation hypnotherapy CDs
- ✓ Don't eat too late. Try not to eat at least two hours before bed as the digestion process can disturb sleep.

Exercise: Food and exercise diary

Over the next two weeks keep a diary of what you eat and how much exercise you take. Gradually over that time increase your exercise, practise the breathing exercises and change your food balance to more healthy food. Make one change a day. Below is a one week version, please do visit www.UoLearn.com to download your full 14 day version.

Date	Food	Exercise	Observations

Personal reflection – the importance of good nutrition and hydration

Managing stress effectively requires a holistic approach i.e. looking at the whole and that includes good nutrition, exercise and hydration to maintain good health. We have looked at how and why we get stressed and some tools to manage it but it is also crucial to look after yourself properly as one of the first things that suffers during stressful times is health.

Your health can suffer because the immune system may not be as efficient as usual which makes us more susceptible to illness. Also many people tend to respond to stress with unhealthy activities such as eating more junk food, drinking more alcohol or caffeine and smoking more. So we can make the problem much worse as these activities can increase our overall physiological stress levels.

Some people also let their exercise routine lapse when they are too busy or too stressed which means that we have less energy or don't sleep properly causing even more issues in how we feel and function on a day to day basis. It can get very much like a vicious cycle.

I found all of these were things that I did when stress levels were high in my life and I am still aware that I could easily slip back into that vicious cycle if I am not careful. I learned that small changes brought about big results and that not putting pressure on myself with thoughts like I have to go to the gym, I have to drink 2 litres of water, I have to eat x amount of food etc. really helped. I made small changes over time and hope that some of the tips people gave me and others that I discovered along the way may help you too.

Here are some of my suggestions and things I do that could help you to stay healthy during times of stress:

✓ Measure your water into a water bottle or flask and carry it with you - sip it throughout the day. This will remind you to drink enough water each day and you will also see if this isn't happening as you will have some left at the end of the day.

✓ Drink a glass of water when you wake up each morning to help hydrate and get alert.

✓ Switch to herbal teas or hot water with lime or lemon – all of these are hydrating.

✓ Cook large amounts of food and freeze it in portion sizes – this is your own version of fast food. You can make chillis, currys, broths, soups, bolognaise, stews or anything you can think of and simply defrost and reheat with some veg, pasta or rice. Just as quick as a microwave dinner but you know exactly what is in it and it's healthy.

✓ Cook twice as much and take it for your lunch the next day.

✓ You can make a huge batch of sandwiches and freeze them in handy bags. Just take out a bag each morning and it will be defrosted by lunchtime. All cooked meat will freeze well, as will cheese and tinned fish. Salad does not freeze well so take it and add it at lunch time.

✓ Wash and chop up lots of different fruit and make a big bowl of fruit salad – you can grab a portion each day and it will last for a few days.

✓ Snack on nuts (unsalted) and seeds instead of bread and biscuits.

✓ Raw veggies and dips make a good treat.

✓ Grains like quinoa make a good and speedy alternative to brown rice and are just as healthy.

✓ If you feel tired and don't want to exercise just do 10 minutes and then decide from there. If you can do more go ahead and if not stop and rest. 10 minutes is better than nothing and will still help you to feel more energised.

Session 6

Integration of Strategies
and Action Plan

"Success will never be a big step in the future,
success is a small step taken just now."
Jonatan Mårtensson

Session 6 :
Integration of Strategies and Action Plan

As we near the end of this stress programme, I'd like you to consider what you've already learnt and what changes you've started to apply on both a conscious and unconscious level.

Think about all the strategies we've covered. Which feel right for you? And which can you adapt quickly and easily into your life? Remember, sometimes the smaller changes can have the biggest results.

Objectives:

When you've explored this chapter, you will be able to:

✓ put what you've learnt into perspective

✓ decide which stress-beating strategies are right for you

✓ use our four-step process to make positive and effective changes

Tools in this chapter

✓ Summary and tips – reminders of twelve key points and strategies

✓ Life areas assessment tool – document to gain awareness of your starting point

✓ Sun diagrams (or mini-mindmaps) – to use to decide what you want to change and how

✓ Well formed outcome – twenty one questions to ensure what you want to achieve/change is right for you in every way

✓ Goal setting chart – use to write your goals and plan the action you are going to take to be proactive in managing stress

Summary and tips to beat stress

During this programme, we've asked you to look at:

➢ Your beliefs and how they help or hinder you
➢ What reality you create
➢ Whether you actually are the cause of most of your stress.

We've discussed:

What stress actually is:

➢ How it can affect and harm us both physically and mentally
➢ How important attitudes are
➢ How they affect us and others immensely

We've shown you:

➢ Ways to change and manage the amount of stress in your life
➢ How to challenge and change negative beliefs and thought and behaviour patterns
➢ How to take an inward approach to look at change and stress strategies. (Remember – the only thing we can control is ourselves)
➢ How to embrace change rather than meet it with resistance

We've addressed the best way to maintain good health with:

➢ Nutrition
➢ Supplementation
➢ Hydration
➢ Exercise
➢ Relaxation

The next step is to put it all together and commit to making changes. What changes are you willing to make? Remember this is your CHOICE and from this point on, it's up to you!

What quality of life and living do you choose?

In a moment we're going to look at a quick goal-setting exercise to get you started. This will give you a clear direction and enable you to choose your own personal stress strategy from all the ones presented to you during this programme. Before we start goal setting, let's just have a quick reminder of some of the strategies you can adopt.

Stress Beating Strategies

1. Recognition

Remember that firstly, you need to be aware of stress before you can do anything about it.

Use the stress curve (stress versus performance diagram in session 2) to keep track of where you are and make sure that you're maintaining a healthy optimum balance or moving in the right direction.

Also, be aware of how stress affects your physical body as well as your behaviour and performance. Watch out for indicators of stress so you can do something sooner rather than later, reaching the burn out point is not a good option.

You now have the tools to spot your own stress, and assess and manage its levels.

2. Beliefs and Attitude

Limiting beliefs can cause stress – and they could easily account for 80 per cent of the stress you're experiencing. The good news is that beliefs are learnt and so can be changed.

You're now aware of some of your limiting beliefs and some powerful techniques for change:

➤ Compounding
➤ Positive thinking
➤ Reframing

Practise these skills, as they do work and they'll become much easier.

Remember how the cognitive process works: you don't have to believe new desired beliefs immediately, just create a new habit and the rest will come easily – trust me!

3. Embrace change

Change is a part of life; there's no escaping it. Yes, it can be scary as it's the unknown, but the worst rarely happens. Look at change as an exciting or good thing and it will help to significantly reduce daily stress. Resist change and you will experience stress and anxiety – plus the change may be forced upon you anyway.

4. Analyse your current position and desired position

Ask yourself good questions such as:

➢ How much do I suffer from stress and why?

➢ How does stress affect me personally?

➢ What does that mean to me/cost me?

➢ Why am I here/in this situation?

➢ What have I done or not done?

➢ What are my beliefs about this and are they the best for me?

➢ How could my thoughts and behaviour be adapted to get to where I want to be or to feel differently about situations?

➢ What changes do I need to make and how can I make them?

5. Healthy eating and hydration

Good nutrition and hydration are essential during everyday life but even more so during stressful times. Be kind to yourself!

Adrenaline and other hormones and chemicals released during times of stress reduce the strength of your body's immune and digestive systems. You're more prone to illness, ulcers, irritable bowel syndrome and a whole host of physical problems during periods of stress. Correct hydration and nutrition in times of stress will protect your body and keep your immune system strong.

➤ What small changes can you make to improve your eating habits?

➤ How can you ensure you drink enough water each day?

➤ How can you reduce food and drinks that can stress your body further or dehydrate you?

➤ What things can you put into place to make this easy for you to continue and make it a life long change?

> Drink two litres of water a day. Sip it throughout the day. For a really refreshing drink, try adding lemon or ginger to hot water. Or pour boiling water on fresh mint or lemon balm and infuse.

6. Exercise

Exercise is excellent for expressing stress and negative energy appropriately. It's also a great anti-stress strategy, helping rid toxins from your body, keeping your immune system strong and releasing endorphins to make you feel good.

Remember to exercise everyday, even if only for 10 minutes, and to make it fun and pain free.

7. Relax

Relaxation has been described as nature's tranquilliser.

Only the lucky few can really relax instinctively; the rest of us have to learn how, especially how to breathe properly.

Regular relaxation or meditation trains your body and mind to quickly relax and unwind to leave you refreshed and energised.

Discover the peace and tranquillity within yourself, even if the world is crazy around you.

8. Breathe

Remember to breathe properly.

We've covered lots of breathing techniques to be used at different times, suitable for every event. Practise them and use them. You'll be surprised how much of a difference they can make to how you think and feel.

9. Seek Help

You don't have to handle stress alone. Sometimes seeking help is the best thing to do.

Stress can be greatly reduced by talking it over with someone you trust. This may be your partner, a close friend or colleague or possibly a professional counsellor or coach.

Talking releases the pressures, especially if you're too close to a situation to remain objective or it's an emotionally charged situation. Others can help you see things from a different perspective and help you to make positive changes.

10. Manage yourself and your time

When your workload seems overwhelming, remember:

➢ Some things can always be set aside until later
➢ Concentrate on one particular job at a time and work at it until it's finished
➢ Avoid pressure on yourself by acknowledging that you're only able to achieve so much
➢ Learn to say 'no' when you're under pressure

11. Get a good night's sleep

Quality sleep will always help you to cope with stress. Lack of sleep leaves us feeling weary, irrational and emotional which will magnify a stressful situation.

➢ Prioritise your sleep
➢ Avoid anything that is stressful or stimulating as bedtime approaches
➢ Keep caffeine and alcohol intake to a minimum
➢ Take a lavender bath
➢ Drink camomile tea
➢ Listen to relaxation or hypnotherapy CDs

12. Make a plan, take action

Do something about it!

➢ Use what you have learnt and apply it
➢ Practise it to create new positive habits and behaviours
➢ Set goals and take action
➢ Review goals and changes often to ensure you're still going in the right direction for you
➢ Re-read and complete this programme many times – each time there will be a different outcome, for different reasons

Choose to take positive control of your life.

Goal setting and plans

Step-by-step to positive control

Our straightforward four-step process will help you get to the heart of the matter and create specific, effective actions for change.

✓ The life areas assessment tool to decide where to start making changes

✓ Mindmaps to pinpoint action for improvement

✓ Well formed outcomes to make sure you're choosing the right goals

✓ Goal-setting charts for strategy and detailed tactics

Step 1: The life areas assessment tool or How happy are you?

To help you to decide where to start when making changes to anything, take a look at where you are now and what issues you're currently dealing with. The life areas assessment tool below divides life into 12 broad areas so that you can identify how happy you feel with each. If any areas don't apply, feel free to ignore them as it won't make a difference to the exercise.

Choose a number between 0 and 10 to rate how you feel about the life areas below:
0 means you're desperately unhappy with the situation or find it very stressful.
10 means you feel no stress and you're extremely happy.

	0	1	2	3	4	5	6	7	8	9	10
Finances	☹	○	○	○	○	☺	○	○	○	○	☺
Career/job	☹	○	○	○	○	☺	○	○	○	○	☺
Mental health	☹	○	○	○	○	☺	○	○	○	○	☺
Physical health	☹	○	○	○	○	☺	○	○	○	○	☺
Friends	☹	○	○	○	○	☺	○	○	○	○	☺
Family	☹	○	○	○	○	☺	○	○	○	○	☺
Parenting	☹	○	○	○	○	☺	○	○	○	○	☺
Partner	☹	○	○	○	○	☺	○	○	○	○	☺
Personal dev.	☹	○	○	○	○	☺	○	○	○	○	☺
Fun, recreation	☹	○	○	○	○	☺	○	○	○	○	☺
Home	☹	○	○	○	○	☺	○	○	○	○	☺
Spirituality	☹	○	○	○	○	☺	○	○	○	○	☺

Your scores should give you an idea which areas need the most work.

It's important to note that you're not necessarily aiming for everything being 10. For some people a lower figure is sufficient and the numbers and their significance are relative to the individual, anyway.

If your numbers differ wildly – some high figures along with some very low figures – that's indicative of a lack of balance in life. Your aim is to have a **healthy balance** which is then maintained, throughout all of the life areas.

For example, let's say you want to focus on PHYSICAL HEALTH. You might decide that your main issues are that you have been so busy and so stressed that you have not been exercising and that you would like to change this. Or perhaps you have been drinking lots of coffee and not much water. Suitable goals would be as below.

Remember:

Make your goals positive – 'I will have 1 cup of coffee per day and drink a litre of water throughout the day, every day.'

Be clear and specific – rather than say 'I need to exercise more', say 'I will walk 20 minutes every Monday, Wednesday and Friday morning'

Exercise: Choose the areas you want to work on. They could be the ones with the lowest scores, or the area that is the most stressful at the moment. List the issues you've got with those areas and write down goals that will turn those issues around.

Step 2: Mindmaps or sun diagrams

Once you have chosen your goals, create sun diagrams for each one to identify the actions you need to take.

Create sun diagrams (or mini-mindmaps) for each goal to identify the actions you need to take:

1. Take a piece of plain paper and draw a circle in the middle.

2. Write the name of the goal you've chosen in the circle.

3. Then draw lines from the circle to the outer sides of the paper so it looks a little like a kids drawing of a sun.

4. Brainstorm ideas to make that goal happen.

5. List any and every idea you have.

6. If you fill all the lines add a complete set of new ones all the way around - if your mind sees blank lines it will search the corners to find something to go on them.

Include:

✓ Things that you could do

✓ People you could ask for help or you could influence

✓ Any other resources you can think of

Don't worry if the options don't make sense or you don't know how to do them at this point – just write anything and everything down. All ideas are accepted - you are just brainstorming and can evaluate them later.

Blank sun diagram

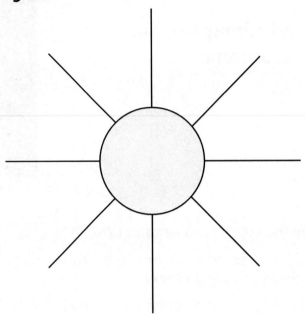

Hint If you need some inspiration, take a look at the example of a filled-in sun diagram below.

> **Exercise: Your own sun diagram.**
>
> Get a large piece of paper and make a sun diagram of the all the possible actions that you could take to achieve one of the goals you have selected in step 1.

Now look over the sun diagram and select those options you're going to use, that make sense and that you feel you can do. When you've selected lots of options and action-points to achieve your desired goal, you're almost ready to fill out the goal setting process. However, before you do, it's important to check that the goal you have chosen is right for you in every way.

Transfer your goal to the well formed outcome process (step 3) and work through the questions to ensure it is a goal you really want to achieve.

Some people select goals they think are good for them without realising they might have to give things up or make sacrifices to achieve them. If they knew, they'd probably rather not aim for that goal and would prefer to choose another.

For example, if you wanted to be a millionaire: it sounds really good, but have you considered how much extra time you'd have to work, perhaps doing more than one job? Or how much you'd need to focus on saving rather than spending money on social activities or holidays? Or that the time working extra hours might have a negative impact on your relationship with children, family and friends?

Transfer your goal to the well-formed outcome process and work through the questions to ensure it is a goal you really want to achieve.

Step 3: Well formed outcome

A well formed outcome is a goal that has been questioned, researched and deeply considered, until it is clear and specific.

When you create well formed outcomes, you look at all the possibilities – good and bad, realistic or unrealistic – so you can make the right decisions, and make it easier to achieve your goals.

Use this checklist to make sure your goals are exactly what you want – and to make sure they're clear and realistic.

Here's an example to give you an idea of how it works:

Well formed outcome example:

1. State the goal or desired outcome positively.
   To achieve a grade 5 pay rise.

2. Is it specific or could you define it more, is it measurable?
   Yes.

3. Can you achieve it by yourself?
   Yes, but I would like help from my manager too.

4. Is the goal positive and ethical to benefit you or others around you, i.e. does it have a positive intention?
   Yes, it will benefit me and my family.

5. How will you know when you have it? How will you feel?
   I will feel I have achieved something I worked hard for and be very happy.

6. Why don't you have it now? Has anything stopped you?
I haven't had enough experience in the past, but feel I am ready now. Perhaps I also needed the confidence to apply.

7. How big a goal is it? Do you need to break it up into smaller goals?
I need to pass the exam first and then apply for the grading, so 2 smaller goals are required.

8. What are all the steps you need to take?
Study for my exam in June.
Pass the exam.
Speak to my manager and tell her I want to apply for the grading.
Ask for her help, support and recommendation.
Apply for the grading.
Get an interview.
Pass the interview.
Get the grading and pay rise.

9. When will you take the first step?
Today, I will email to register for the exam in June.

10. When will you complete it all?
I will have completed all the other steps by December.

11. Are there any other ways to get it?
If I don't pass the exam I can re-sit it in September but if I fail that I will have to wait until June next year. There is no way to get the promotion without passing the exam.

12. What resources do you currently have (physical, emotional, mental, spiritual, financial, knowledge, skills, assistance etc.)?
I have support from my partner and the time to study, the desire and determination to achieve it.

13. What resources will you need?
I will need the agreement and support of my line manager.

14. What will you need to give up to have it? How will it affect you (friends, work, relationships, lifestyle etc)?
I will have to give up my weekends to study which is time with my friends and family, i.e. my social time.

15. What will happen if you don't get it? How will you feel?
    If I don't get it I will keep trying until I do, I will feel disappointed.

16. What will happen if you do get it? How will you feel?
    I will have better future prospects and more money coming in each month so we can have a holiday away and more treats. I will feel fantastic and proud of myself.

17. If you don't get it, will you lose out on anything?
    If I don't get it I will lose out on the money but also feel disappointed. I won't feel that I have achieved my goal and taken control of my life.

18. If you do get it, will you lose out anything?
    I won't lose out on anything.

19. What will having it give to you? For what purpose do you want it?
    I want it for my achievement, better prospects and more financial security.

20. Will achieving this goal enhance your life and/or others around you?
    Yes, mine and my family.

21. Is it a worthwhile goal to aim to achieve? Do you still want to achieve this goal?
    Yes, it is worthwhile and I am going to do it.

Exercise: Well formed outcome

Work through the 21 questions with your chosen goal.

Remember you can download a copy of this from the website. (www.UoLearn.com)

Well formed outcome:

1. State the goal or desired outcome positively.

....
....
....

2. Is it specific or could you define it more, is it measurable?

....
....
....

3. Can you achieve it by yourself?

....
....
....

4. Is the goal positive and ethical to benefit you or others around you i.e. does it have a positive intention?

....
....
....

5. How will you know when you have it? How will you feel?

....
....
....

6. Why don't you have it now? Has anything stopped you?

....
....
....

7. How big a goal is it?
   Do you need to break it into smaller goals?

....
....
....

8. What are all the steps you need to take?

....
....
....

9. When will you take the first step?

....
....
....

10. When will you complete it all?

....
....
....

11. Are there any other ways to get it?

....
....
....

12. What resources do you currently have (physical, emotional, mental, spiritual, financial, knowledge, skills, assistance etc.)?

13. What resources will you need?

14. What will you need to give up to have it?
    How will it affect you (friends, work, relationships, lifestyle)?

15. What will happen if you don't get it?
    How will you feel?

16. What will happen if you do get it?
    How will you feel?

17. If you don't get it, will you lose out on anything?

....

....

....

18. If you do get it, will you lose out anything?

....

....

....

19. What will having it give to you?
    For what purpose do you want it?

....

....

....

20. Will achieving this goal enhance your life and/or others around you?

....

....

....

21. Is it a worthwhile goal to aim to achieve?
    Do you still want to achieve this goal?

....

....

....

If you're happy with this goal, you can now continue to the goal setting process.

Step 4: Goal setting chart

This will detail your own personal stress strategy and ensure you keep on track – make sure you look at it and update it weekly or monthly.

It's not set in stone and can be changed, so don't worry too much if you miss a target date (these could be a day, week, month, year or years). You may even decide to erase some goals and add new ones as you go along.

Any large goals may need to be reduced into smaller goals working towards one big goal; if so you can put this as the title for the whole sheet.

Goals can be wide and varied as different things cause stress for different people. Examples of goals chosen by people we've done this with in the past include:

➢ family and relationship issues to be resolved
➢ job interviews and exams
➢ conflict and issues at home or work
➢ self-belief and confidence issues
➢ time management issues
➢ defined goals such as passing driving test
➢ improving health goals
➢ weight issues
➢ money issues
➢ issues associated with change.

Your goals can be anything you wish, large or small – all are important.

Remember to give yourself a reward for each goal achieved, because you deserve it!

Goal setting criteria:

✓ Have **target dates** by which you will achieve your goals – be specific with dates.

✓ **Review them daily** – put them in your diary or on your wall and read every day.

✓ Make them **specific**, **detailed and** well defined.

✓ Have a means of **measuring progress** towards achievement – you can assess whether you're achieving or moving towards achieving them, or not.

✓ Choose a **reward or treat** for every goal, to be enjoyed when achieved, this doesn't have to cost money.

✓ Set them **without limits**, no matter how large – dream big, choose anything you want.

✓ **Chunk** into smaller goals if necessary – if it's a large goal, make it into smaller goals which when achieved make up the achievement of the large goal.

✓ Have a **defined support infrastructure** – ask for help, you don't have to do it all by yourself!

Goal setting document:

This is how to make sure you cover all the criteria in the list.

A blank version can be downloaded from the website www.UoLearn.com

Goal		
Action points		
Why and what benefit		
Who can help and how		
Date to be achieved		
Results and actions so far + / -		
Date actually achieved		
Reward		
Advice for next time		

GOAL SETTING

Here's is an example of a goals chart created to stop smoking and apply for and secure a new job or promotion.

Goal	To be a non-smoker	Get promoted to senior leader
Action points	Book in to see doctor Buy Patches Ask everyone to support me	Research the post Speak to my manager Apply for the position Practise interview skills Get a new suit
Why and what benefit	Health, save money, be happy and proud of myself	Happier, more money, better hours, challenge
Who can help and how	Partner, Friends, Colleagues, reminding me, helping me find other activities	Manager, advice Partner, support Colleagues
Date to be achieved	25th March	1st April
Results and actions so far + / -	Cut back to 5 a day last month	Applied for job No success meeting with manager
Date actually achieved	30th March	30th May
Reward	Put money saved towards holiday	Celebrate by going out for a family meal
Advice for next time	None - there won't be a next time. I'm a non-smoker now.	Needed more to time to achieve all points i.e. took longer than I expected.

Personal Reflection –
setting goals and making positive changes

We started this programme with information on what stress is and how to spot it, then we progressed to identifying your start point and then straight into lots of strategies to combat and manage stress. Now, you're at the point where you commit to making positive changes for yourself. It would be such a shame for you to have come so far and not make any changes. This is the time to take small steps to make big changes to your life and you now have the tools to do it.

Goal setting is a way of putting your dreams and wishes onto paper and exploring ways of achieving them. When you write down goals you are far more likely to achieve them and it makes it much more real because you then have a target to aim for. Please continue to set your own goals and continue to develop and monitor your goals. It can make such a huge difference to being proactive in not just managing stress but taking control of the direction of your life. Coaching covers many different styles of goal setting and change work. If this kind of thing interests you or you want to know more then we have another book called Coaching Skills Training Course (www.UoLearn.com) which you can use to learn to self-coach or coach others.

Enjoy setting your goals and taking control of your life, it can be anything you desire.

Farewell and Thank You!

Farewell

We really hope you've enjoyed working through this programme with us, and that you're enjoying opening your mind to an abundance of options!

So, finally ...

✓ Pick the strategies, solutions and resources that suit you best

✓ Apply them consistently

✓ Practise

✓ Believe that you can be in control

✓ Be patient and take it one step at a time for real lasting change

✓ Remember, this is your choice and your quality of life.

We've given you signposts, ideas and, hopefully, inspiration – only you can make the difference.

So now it's over to you!

If you've enjoyed this programme, you'll find the list of our other programmes at our website: www.realifeltd.co.uk

Good luck in the future!

'Why follow the path when you can create your own trail?'

Kathryn Critchley

Notes

Index

Further reading

"Books are the quietest and most constant of friends;
they are the most accessible and wisest of counsellors,
and the most patient of teachers." Charles W. Eliot

Further reading

References

The Structure of Magic, Richard Bandler and John Grinder, Science and Behaviour, (1975)

Thinking Styles: Relationships That Work, Fiona Beddoes-Jones, BJA Associates (1999)

The Complete Idiot's Guide to Managing Stress, Jeff Davidson, Alpha Books, (1999)

Fats that Heal, Fats that Kill, Udo Erasmus, Alive Books (1993)

NLP at Work: The Difference that Makes a Difference in Business, Sue Knight, 2nd Edition, Nicholas Brealey Pub. (2002)

The Bones of The Milk Argument, Financial Times (1999)

Mind Over Mood: Change How You Feel by Changing the Way You Think, Dennis Greenberger and Christine Padessky, The Guilford Press (1995)

New Optimum Nutrition Bible, Patrick Holford, Platkus (2002)

Teaching With the Brain in Mind, Eric Jensen, Association for Supervision and Curriculum Development (1998)

You Are What You Eat, Gillian McKeith, Penguin (2004)

The New Handbook of Cognitive Therapy Techniques, Rian McMullin, WW Norton and co (2000)

Strategic Stress Management: An Organisational Approach, Valerie Sutherland and Cary Cooper, Macmillan (2000)

Cognitive Responses in Persuasion, Richard Petty, Thomas Ostrom and Timothy Bruck, Lawrence Erlbaum Assoc (1981)

The Psychology of Attitudes, M Sherif and H Cantril, Pyschology Review, 52 p295-319 (1945)

The pH Miracle, Robert and Shelly Young, Warner Books (2005)

Adrenal Fatigue, Vicki Wade, www.project-aware.org

Bibliography:

Stress Management

Emotional Intelligence, Daniel Goleman
Conquer Your Stress, Cry Cooper and Stephen Palmer
Living with Stress, Cary Cooper
What's all this Stress? Brenda Davison
Fit for Life, Marilyn and Harvey Diamond
Happiness Now! A Timeless Wisdom for Feeling Good Fast,
Robert Holden
The Care Guide, Michael Jacobs
The Book of Stress Survival, Alix Kirsta
**Positive Under Pressure: How To Be Calm and Effective
When The Heat Is On,** Gael Lindenfield
At Ease With Stress, Wanda Nash
Creating a Balance: Managing Stress, Stephen Palmer, Cary
Cooper and Kate Thomas
The Mental Health Handbook, Trevor Powell
Success Over Stress,: Seven Strategies, Jane Ravell
Unlimited Power, Anthony Robbins

Bullying

Bullying at Work: How to Confront and Overcome It, Andrea
Adams
**Bully in Sight: How to Predict, Resist Challenge and Combat
Workplace Bullying,** Tom Field
Building a Culture of Respect: Managing Bullying at Work,
Noreen Tehrani

Time Management

Better Time Management, Jacqueline Atkinson
First Things First Every Day, Stephen Covey
The Time Management Pocket Book, Ian Fleming
**10 minute Time and Stress Management,: How to Gain an
Extra 10 Hours a Week,** David Lewis

Changing your Thinking

Words That Change Minds: Mastering The Language And Influence, Shelly Rose Charvet, Kendall Hunt (1997)

Influence: The Psychology Of Persuasion, Robert B Cialdini, Collins (1998)

Developing your Influencing skills, L Burton and D Dalley, Universe of Learning (2009)

Seven Habits Of Highly Effective People, Stephen R Covey, Simon and Schuster (1999)

Lateral Thinking, Edward De Bono, Penguin

Thinking Course, Edward De Bono, Petanco (1989)

Strategies Of Genius, Robert Dilts, Meta Publications (1996)

Believe You Can, Clive Gott, (2004)

Excuse Me Your Life Is Waiting, Lynn Grabhorn, Hodder and Staughton (2004)

Turtles All The Way Down, John Grinder and Judith DeLozier, Metamorphous Press (1996)

I'm OK You're OK, Thomas A Harris, Arrow (1995)

Counselling Skills and Theory, Margaret Hough, Hodder and Staughton (2003)

Time Line Therapy and the Basis Personality, Tad James and Wyatt Woodsmall, Meta Publications

Raw Energy, Susanna and Lesley Kenton, Vermilion (1994)

The NLP Coach, Ian McDermot and Wendy Jago, Piatkus (2001)

Notes From A Friend, Anthony Robbins, Simon and Schuster (1996)

Power To Influence, Anthony Robbins, CD Set

The Psychobiology of Mind Body Healing, Ernest Rossi, W W Norton and co (1993)

The 11th Element, Robert Scheinfeld, Wiley (2003)

Presenting Magically, Tad James and David Shephard, Crown House (2004)

Understanding Misunderstandings, Nancy Slessenger, Vine House (2003)

Permission To Succeed, Noah St John, Health Communications (1999)

The Psychology of Achievement, Brian Tracy, CD set, (1988)

Coaching for Performance, John Whitmore, Nicholas Brealey Publishing (2002)

Universe of Learning books

"The things I want to know are in books; my best friend is
the man who'll get me a book I ain't read."

Abraham Lincoln

About the publishers

Universe of Learning Limited is a small publisher based in the UK with production in England and America. Our authors are all experienced trainers or teachers who have taught their skills for many years. We are actively seeking qualified authors and if you visit the authors section on www.UoLearn.com you can find out how to apply.

If you would like any of our current authors (including Kathryn Critchley) to speak at your event please do visit their own websites (for Kathryn it's www.realifeltd.co.uk) or email them through the author section of the UoLearn site.

If you would like to purchase larger numbers of books then please do contact us (sales@UoLearn.com). We give discounts from 5 books upwards. For larger volumes we can also quote for changes to the cover to accommodate your company logo and to the interior to brand it for your company.

All our books are written by teachers, trainers or people well experienced in their roles and our goal is to help people develop their skills with a well structured range of exercises.

If you have any feedback about this book or other topics that you'd like to see us cover please do contact us at support@UoLearn.com.

Keep Learning!

Coaching Skills Training Course

Your toolkit to coaching yourself and others, with exercises and scripts

ISBN: 978-1-84937-019-6, from www.UoLearn.com

This book gives you an easy to follow structure to design inspiring coaching sessions.

✓ An easy to follow 5 step model to guide you through the coaching process.
✓ Exercises will help you enhance your skills
✓ Work at your own pace to increase your ability
✓ How to use NLP in your coaching
✓ Over 25 ready to use ideas

A toolbox of ideas to help you become a great coach.

Speed Writing Skills Training Course

Speedwriting for faster note taking and dictation, an alternative to shorthand to help you take notes.

Easy exercises to learn faster writing in just 6 hours. Free downloadable Dictionary and Workbook.

ISBN 978-1-84937-011-0, from www.UoLearn.com

✓ "The principles are very easy to follow, and I am already using it to take notes."
✓ "BakerWrite is the easiest shorthand system I have come across. Having studied all the major shorthand systems and other speed writing courses, I find BakerWrite a sheer delight."
✓ "I will use this system all the time."
✓ "Your system is so easy to learn and use."

Report Writing

An easy to follow format for writing business reports

ISBN 978-1-84937-036-3, from www.UoLearn.com

This book makes report writing a step by step process for you to follow every time you have a report to write.

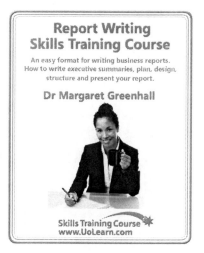

✓ How to set objectives using 8 simple questions
✓ Easy to follow flow chart
✓ How to write an executive summary
✓ How to layout and structure the report
✓ Help people remember what they read

Developing Your Influencing Skills,

How to influence people by increasing your credibility, trustworthiness and communication skills

ISBN: 978-1-84937-022-6, from www.UoLearn.com

What are the characteristics that make some people more influential than others?

This book will give you the keys to successfully increase your influence at work and at home.
In this book you will discover how to:
✓ Decide what your influencing goals are
✓ Find ways to increase your credibility rating
✓ Develop stronger and more trusting relationships
✓ Inspire others to follow your lead
✓ Become a more influential communicator

This book is packed with case studies, exercises and practical tips to help develop the traits required to become more influential.

Successful Minute Taking Meeting the Challenge

How to prepare, write and organise agendas and minutes of meetings

ISBN 978-1-84937-040-0, from www.UoLearn.com

✓ Becoming more confident in your role
✓ A checklist of what to do
✓ Help with layout and writing skills
✓ Learn what to include in minutes
✓ How to work well with your chairperson

Learn to be an excellent meeting secretary.

How to Start a Business as a Private Tutor

ISBN 978-1-84937-029-5, from www.UoLearn.com

This book, by a Lancashire based author, shows you how to set up your own business as a tutor.

✓ Packed with tips and stories
✓ How to get started - what to do and buy
✓ How to attract clients and advertise
✓ Free printable forms, ready to use
✓ Advice on preparing students for exams

Practical and Effective Performance Management

How excellent leaders manage their staff and teams for top performance

ISBN: 978-1-84937-037-0, from www.UoLearn.com

✓ Five key ideas to understanding performance
✓ A clear four step model
✓ A large, wide ranging choice of tools
✓ Practical exercises and action planning
✓ Develop your leadership skills

A toolbox of ideas to help you become a better leader.